BAPTISM AS A WAY OF LIFE

Klara Tammany

CHURCH
PUBLISHING
INCORPORATED

Church Publishing
19 East 34th Street
New York, NY 10016

Cover design: Jennifer Kopec, 2Pug Design
Chinese character calligraphy: Nguyen Lam
Mediations on Chinese characters: Thomas Chu
Watercolors of water themes: Stewart White
Chapter title page photos of loons: Klara Tammany
Book design: Linda Brooks

A record of this book is available from the Library of Congress.

ISBN-13: 978-1-64065-459-4 (paperback)
ISBN-13: 978-1-64065-460-0 (ebook)

Permissions

Contents

Dedication and Acknowledgments

The people of
Trinity Episcopal Church,
"A doorway to compassion and courage."
And the Tree Street neighborhood
of Lewiston, Maine, in which it resides.

This book has been written by Klara Tammany and friends, many friends. Those of us working in the field of religious education and formation often say that none of us has an original idea. Everything we have learned and done is at least inspired by someone else, if not copied outright. This resource is no exception. It has been created directly or indirectly by a wide community of mentors and colleagues, over many years, in a variety of places. Where I have remembered a source, I have given credit. My apologies for instances that have been overlooked. May the following acknowledgments fill any holes.

Ted Eastman, and his book, *The Baptizing Community,* clarified my early thoughts. It is upon his urging that this book came to be. The ideas were first tried at St. Paul's Church, in Brunswick, Maine, and then refined as part of my graduate thesis at Boston College. The influence of three teachers there, Parker Palmer, Maria Harris and Tom Groome, along with many other mentors shaped my subsequent ministry. Many of those who were listed in the first edition are now among the saints, as are both my parents. Several colleagues from those earlier years contributed stories to the book. Their names appear alongside their texts. Ongoing, deep gratitude to them and to colleagues then in the Diocese of Maryland and elsewhere, who submitted quotes, poems, prayers or appended materials.

Church Publishing took a chance on this book in 2002 and just as a I was about to retire, asked to re-print it. I remain profoundly grateful to Johnny Ross, the original editor who empowered me to write with heart, Stewart White for his drawings that so contemplatively capture the images of water, and Linda Brooks for the evocative layout. Together we created a book that looked like what it was trying to say.

Thank you to Sharon Pearson and Wendy Barrie for advocating a twentieth anniversary updated edition of *Living Water.* Deep appreciation also to Kathy Bozzuti-Jones. One of her stories graced the original edition. In this edition, she helped identify weak or outdated spots and in some of those places contributed new pieces. Many thanks to Peter Bals for his gracious work to help me get the necessary permissions.

Due to copywrite issues some quotes have been removed, but new stories and other content have been added. The layout is now more condensed to make the printing less costly. The appended resources have been removed as they are long out of date, and everything these days easily can be found and shared on the internet.

The Epilogue has been greatly expanded with a focus on the new vow about the environment, *"Will you cherish the wondrous works of God, and protect the beauty and integrity of all creation?"* Friends from my parish, Trinity Episcopal Church in Lewiston, Maine, offer beginning content, but it is not a full chapter. You are invited dear readers, to crowd source the rest of the content by sharing your stories and ideas for this vow, along with resources and suggestions for other chapters, on the Living Water web page: http://www.livingwaterbaptism.net.

This new edition is dedicated to that small faith community of Trinity Church, and the Tree Street neighborhood in Lewiston, Maine, in which it resides. Stories about the parish appear in chapter five about proclaiming the Good News of God as well as the Epilogue.

The members of Trinity are like my family. For decades, in a steadfast commitment, they have shown the power of a living faith as described in this book. After years in parish, diocesan, and national ministry, now an elder, single woman, my life is grounded with them, very locally. I serve in retirement as one of the resident mentors in the Sophia's House community, just two blocks from the parish and one of its outgrowths.

What has transpired has been challenging, and has led me to a deeper, more personal understanding of a lived, personal, practical theology. Almost every day, an encounter with someone on the street, whose name I know, has taught me about the reality of injustice, the importance of dignity, the need for respect, the potential for peace, the call to seek and serve Christ, and the power of Love in so doing.

As I write, we are nearly two years into the pandemic. It is unclear how or when we will come out of this period of fear and isolation. The current situation raises uncertainties about the future of our culture, while the devastation of the environment rages on, and racism and inequality continue to run rampant.

These times beg the question, what does this new reality mean for the Church? For example, I found myself struggling at Easter 2019 with the fact that Eucharist was not accessible to any of us during a stressful emergency, even on the highest of Holy days. I wondered, in the words of Wesley Frensdorff, when the church would stop holding Eucharist hostage to an ordained elite?! I also hope that future prayer book revisions include the new vow to care for this fragile earth, our island home, all of its creatures and forms of life.

A year ago, The Very Rev. Van Gardiner died. During my years in Maryland, he was the Dean of The Cathedral of the Incarnation in Baltimore, and was a dear friend and mentor. Much of what he taught, both by word and example, is in this book, including a story about the

Cathedral, and a story by Van himself. His optimism, exuberant way of living, and deep ability to love and care (especially for children and the poor), infected us all.

As Van's children reminded us at the memorial service this fall, in the midst of pandemic, we can still hear his cheer: "Who has it better than we do?" The answer… "NO-body!" That proclamation captures the truth that whatever emerges, this one thing we know: God is still God, and that God is with us still. We also know that the Good News of God in Christ is ever more needed, as are small communities of believers who practice a faith-filled way of life.

Van also taught me that if you have a call to serve, and it seems impossible, just begin to act as if it has already happened. Always first say "YES." and instead of doubting or questioning, simply ask "HOW?" Then wait and watch and listen, and the way will appear. That advice has never failed, and has made miracles happen.

The more we can live that way, practicing what we preach, and holding each other accountable, the better. For all those who, like Van, continually show me the way, I am truly grateful.

Glory to God whose power, working in us, can do infinitely more than we can ask or imagine …

Klara Tammany
Advent 1, 2021

Prologue

"This is no trifling matter for you, but rather your very life..."
— Deuteronomy 32:47

There is a mystical bird—a symbol of wilderness and solitude—that lives on North Woods lakes in the summer. It is commonly called a loon. Cree Indians named it "Mookwa," meaning "the Spirit of the Northern Waters." About the size of a goose, it has a long, pointed bill and, in the summer, has distinctive black and white plumage. Loons feed on small fish and so are skilled underwater swimmers, often staying down for several minutes and going as far as a hundred yards in one dive. If you have ever been lucky enough to be swimming and have one pop up right in front of you, you know they have brilliant, ruby-red eyes. Their calls are hauntingly ancient and range from an eerie wail to a screeching yodel, or melodic tremolo. The lonely sounds echo across lakes, especially in the quiet nights and early mornings. The first time you hear them, your heart quivers. You feel as if you will never be the same again.

A prehistoric species that is sixty million years old, loons have existed in North America longer than any other bird. They mate for life, which can be twenty to thirty years. If lucky, they have one or two chicks each season. A loon's territorial needs are specific and great. Each pair requires its own pond (the Maine word for a smaller lake)—that is, except before migration, when they gather in parties to socialize. While kayaking one misty early morning on Sand Pond, I found myself suddenly in the midst of their social mysteries—seven of them dancing and singing to a double echo of themselves from nearby hills. They had chosen their spot carefully. What a marvelously joyful way to begin a day!

Unfortunately, because of human incursions, the loon is now listed as a protected species. As a result, they are carefully watched. The arrival of the loons after each long winter is highly anticipated and marks the turn of spring. Those of us who live on the lake sometimes place a friendly wager on the date of their return. We know where the regular island nesting sites are hidden, and we monitor them from a safe distance. These vigils are often the topic of neighborly conversation.

Similar vigils and conversations take place all over the state. There are "loon counts" every summer. On an appointed day, designated people all across Maine are asked to call in the number of baby loons that have been spotted. Loon lovers eagerly await the report on the evening news and celebrate successes. On our pond, we once went for two years without a single chick sighting, and we mourned the loss. One probable cause, we were told, was that—since loons nest very near shore and since the water was unusually high both springs—the nests may have flooded.

Because loons are such captivating creatures, when one is near, you stop and watch—as I did one midsummer day. There, not far from shore, was a mother loon and her chick. The mother dove down into the water. She came up with a fish and went to give it to the young one. This time though, before connecting, she dropped it. She went under again. Came up. Offered another fish, and dropped it. Again. And again. Over and over again. Into the water. Up with food that was then released. At first I thought the mother and chick just missed each other, but after watching this ritual for ten or twenty (or was it thirty?) minutes, it dawned on me—she was trying to get the chick to fish for itself! No effort was spared. If the young loon could not fend for itself by the time the lake froze over, it would not survive. And not only did that chick's life depend on learning how to fish, the entire protected species depended on it.

Every single one counted ... in more ways than I could comprehend at the time ...

My encounter with the loon, on that small, quiet lake in Maine many years ago, marked the beginning of a personal and vocational transformation. The following fall, just before All Saints' Day, I was gearing up for our parish's intergenerational baptism preparation program—a day in which children and adults interacted and explored the meaning of baptism. For some reason, I was also preparing a church school lesson based on a Moses story. The passage was from Deuteronomy 32, near the end of the wilderness journey. In the story, Moses sits all the people down in front of him and recites a song which tells the story of their life with God. Moses ends the song with these words:

> *Take to heart all the words that I am giving in witness*
> *against you today; give them as a command to your*
> *children, so that they may diligently observe all the words*
> *of this law. This is no trifling matter for you, but rather it*
> *is your very life; through it you may live long in the land*
> *that you are crossing over the Jordan to possess.*

As I prepared my lesson, the themes of baptism and Moses' charge to God's people began to merge, and the memory of the loon came back to me. What I was doing began to take on the urgency of the loon teaching her young one to manage on its own. It was no trifling matter!

Introduction

We as Christians, like the loon, are only a generation away from extinction. Since our Christian existence is marked by the water of baptism, how then ought we nurture the faithful so that we all fully live our faith in daily life?

While studying at Boston College, I wrote a paper on baptism. The paper described a program we had created in our parish called "I Will With God's Help." It was based on the Baptismal Covenant questions. The process was intended to prepare candidates for confirmation, reaffirmation and reception.

In the course of research, I found an article titled "Christian Initiation" by the Rt. Rev. Frederick B. Wolfe, the Bishop of Maine, my own bishop! It turned out that he had chaired the committee that prepared the baptismal liturgies for the 1979 Book of Common Prayer. These words caught my attention:

> As in Holy Baptism itself, the proposed initiatory rites begin more than they accomplish.
> It is my conviction that if we take the rites seriously, we may be brought to a radical
> rediscovery of the fullness of Christian life and a deepened theology of Church and Holy Baptism.
> Much lies ahead for us if we take Christian initiation seriously.[1]

I phoned Bishop Wolf, who had just retired, and made an appointment to visit him. We met over tea in his garden and talked.[2] He told me that although the new rites "reflected the church's social and theological awareness in those days," they also helped shape its theology. He saw them as "interim rites," the first steps toward an understanding of baptism that was radically new, yet also ancient. Through these new rites we would continue to sort out our theology and ecclesiology. He was convinced that they would bring great changes, more than we realized.

To help explain, the bishop told me about the traditional principle of *"lex orandi, lex credendi."* It is a phrase that means "The law of praying is the law of believing." It summarized an understanding that prayer forms belief. An expansion suggests the reverse, that prayer, to some extent, is also influenced by doctrine. He then shared a contemporary addition, always implied, but newly articulated: *Lex agendi*, the law of acting. This third piece suggests that life experience (*agendi*) gives power to prayer (*orandi*) and illuminates belief (*credendi*). The three dynamics he insisted, exist in a chicken and egg relationship. Each informs and is informed to some extent by the others.[3]

---

1 Frederick B Wolf, "Christian Initiation," in *Prayer Book Renewal*, ed. Barry H. Evans (New York: Seabury, p. 44).
2 The following is from a conversation with Bishop Wolf, August 1992.
3 For a basic discussion of the principle *lex orandi, lex credendi, lex agendi*, see Kevin Irwin, *Liturgical Theology: A Primer* (Collegeville, MN: Order of St. Benedict, Inc. 1990).

The conversation helped clarify my evolving thoughts. The Latin phrase *"lex orandi, lex credenda, lex agenda"* gave me a way to articulate them. I came to call this connection between prayer, faith, and Christian life/ministry, "practical theology." It became the focus of my graduate thesis, has remained a constant in my vocational pilgrimage, and is the foundation of this book.

Part One: Theology and Theory

Anglicans are a liturgized lot. We are not a confessional church like our more Protestant friends; neither do we have a magisterium. Lacking a Luther, a Calvin, or a papal authority, we have the Prayer Book as our source of identity. Our beliefs are defined and refined through how we worship. The principal of *lex orandi, lex credendi, lex agendi* particularly speaks to us. Historically, our liturgy has been both formative and expressive of belief and life. Our early prayer books—beginning with Thomas Cranmer's—and all subsequent revisions have sought to better manifest that expectation. Rising from the liturgical renewal movement of the mid-twentieth century, the Book of Common Prayer 1979 is the most radical revision to date. It exemplifies the interplay of *orandi, credendi,* and *agendi* through a holistic understanding of liturgy and life, grounded in a baptismal ecclesiology. What are the Prayer Book revisions that Bishop Wolf was so convinced were leading to a "radical rediscovery of the fullness of Christian life, and a deepened theology of Church and Holy Baptism"? And if these indeed are "interim rites"— as he so firmly believed—what changes lie ahead of us?

In its words, arrangement, and composition, the 1979 Prayer Book expresses the new vision of baptism. The service of Holy Baptism is the heart of the Prayer Book. It is placed conspicuously within the Prayer Book texts: following The Great Vigil of Easter (which is itself a significant baptismal addition) and preceding the liturgy for the Eucharist. The three are integral rites. The liturgies, in their textual placement, their theology, and their liturgical actions, reinforce each other: Eucharist is a weekly reminder of baptism; and The Great Vigil includes an annual renewal of our vows. The rubrics reinforce the emphasis on baptism by calling it "full initiation" and saying that it is to be celebrated within the context of the Eucharist, preferably at the Easter Vigil, or on All Saints' Day, Pentecost, or the Baptism of Our Lord. Overall, baptism no longer stands on its own as a private or sporadically performed ritual. Rather, it is to be adequately prepared for and firmly based in community life. Parents and godparents are asked to commit to children's upbringing in the Christian faith, as are the gathered faithful who witness the baptism and promise to support those who are baptized.

In addition to those changes, there is a remarkable expansion of the Baptismal Covenant (BCP, pp. 304–305) and the understanding of ministry in the Catechism (BCP, pp. 855–856). Those previously baptized are called to join the candidates in a profession of faith and life. In the vows, there is no escaping the expectation that baptism is a lifelong commitment with distinct public consequences. Our Catechism supports the baptismal vision with an obvious emphasis on the daily ministry of all God's people. Laity are to "represent Christ and his Church; to bear witness to him wherever they may be; and, according to the gifts given them, to carry on Christ's work of reconciliation in the world; and to take their place in the life, worship, and governance of the Church." This wording sets up an unfortunate dichotomy between laity and those called to ordained ministry, but the intent is later stated: "The duty of *all* Christians is to follow Christ; to come together week by week for corporate worship; and to work, pray, and give for the spread of the kingdom of God" [italics mine].

The Prayer Book texts contain some mixed messages that lead to an imbalance between the actions/words of the liturgies (*orandi*) and belief (*credendi*), an imbalance which then impedes our fully living the vows (*agendi*). The biggest problems are related to the unequal liturgical weight given the rites of baptism and ordination, and the confusion over the purpose of confirmation.

One shift that has already thankfully occurred is that baptism is no longer universally treated as the "entrance rite" required for receiving Eucharist. That practice had become a barrier. In many parishes, including my own, anyone who hungers, is now welcome to receive the bread and wine. Eucharist has slowly and quietly become the entrance point, and those who are fed, who hunger for more, can be baptized.

These and other internal inconsistencies muddy the waters. However, it is beyond the scope of this book to raise the issues of whether we should reconsider our practices of confirmation and how we might adjust or reconfigure our prayer and polity, in general, and our baptismal and ordination liturgies, in particular.[4]

I choose to work from the positive. Given that baptism remains a foundational sacrament, we should understand the implications it has for our lives. Because of the practice of infant baptism, many adults in our church today do not remember their baptism. They need constantly to be reminded of its implications. Others who have not been baptized need those of us who *have* to be clear about its meaning. As we enter further into a post-Christian era, it will only become more crucial that we do so. For all of God's people, we can and must better connect what we practice, proclaim, and pray. We must intentionally and consciously find ways to make baptism a grounding for our lives as Christians. I maintain that, by embodying our tradition as it is, fully and with integrity, we will live in joyous response to God's love and grace. Doing so will also help us discern the changes needed to move constructively forward.

What is a next step? Generally, we must search for what is ecclesially appropriate and culturally consistent today. We must include not just the teaching of content; there must also be

---

4 Some examples: In the Prayers of the People we pray first and separately for bishops, priests, and deacons, and then – in what appears to be descending order of importance – we pray for all *other* ministers. Biddings frequently are worded as requests for God to intercede magically on behalf of those oppressed and in need, instead of as requests that we, as active participants, be given the wisdom and will to respond. Confirmations seems to relegate baptism to the status of a mere first step toward full initiation, with confirmation eventually completing the good work already begun. Although baptism, supposedly, has primacy in the ritual life of Episcopalians, the church does little to ensure that the symbols of baptism are given pride of place in the ongoing life of community. The symbols, the font and the water, are often all but hidden in corners or put away when not in use. The rite of baptism is also overshadowed by the rite or ordination; of the two services, ordination is the more dramatic, so much so that a casual observer of both liturgies probably would conclude that the conferring of holy orders is somehow the more significant of the two.

creative kinds of nurture and formation that are tied to life experience, that are as much of the heart as of the head. It will require an ongoing "cradle-to-grave" effort that is more than Sunday school. Lisa Kimball, a well-known religious educator puts it this way: "Faith formation as we have done it tends to be consistent yet terminal (at about age 14), when it ought to be occasional and lifelong."

Throughout, we can assist members of our faith communities in adopting the Baptismal Covenant as a way of life. By that I mean a regular discipline of prayerfully pondering faith and life experiences in light of baptism—a mystagogy of sorts that never ends. Please note that I am not proposing a practice of "works righteousness" that would create a baptismal litmus test for what we need to do to be holy or saved. I do suggest that we use our baptismal theology as a lens through which we look at our lives, both individually and collectively. It has to do with discerning any tension between our faith and life, and bringing faith and life into greater balance. Two basic questions shape the conversation: What does your life say about your belief? How does your belief in God influence the way you live your life? We have a hint of a baptismal way of life in the renewal of vows that is built into each celebration of Holy Baptism and the Easter Vigil. Those occasions, however, provide only a touchstone. Jean Haldane suggests that our vows become "vain repetition" without "a way to give an account of ourselves before God and one another in the body of Christ." Accountability can happen, she feels, when people share their experiences of daily ministry and reflect on the vows.[5] What if we were intentional about preparing for times when vows are made or affirmed? What if we gave the vows more than simple lip service?

This book, *Living Water: Baptism as a Way of Life*, is one contribution towards a renewed education and formation, based on our baptismal call to vocation. The process aims to bring participants to a deeper understanding of the implications of their baptismal profession of faith. Through theological reflection and discernment focused on the baptismal vows, participants will ask questions of their lives, and be led to some clarity about acting on their faith. The process may lead participants to a formal affirmation or reaffirmation of vows, or to a blessing for a specific ministry. Springs of baptism are freely flowing. It is up to us to drink of the living water, regularly and often. Consider where such an expanded understanding of baptism may lead us.

- **A Baptismal Paradigm and Piety:** A baptismal way of life presupposes that conversion is ongoing, and understands ministry to be truly in keeping with a theology of the priesthood of all believers. We live out of an ecclesiology based in baptism, a "baptismal paradigm" of sorts.[6] A parallel "baptismal piety" supports us in living out faith in the world.[7] It means that all we do—as the church and as individuals—is influenced by our understanding of baptism.

5 Jean Haldane, "Private Faith and Public Responsibility" in *Reshaping Ministry: Essays in Memory of Wesley Frensdorf,* ed Josephine Borgeson and Lynn Wilson (Avada, CO: Jethro Publications, 1990), p. 184.

6 See William Seth Adams, "Decoding the Obvious: Reflections on Baptismal Ministry in the Episcopal Church" in *Baptism and Ministry: Liturgical Studies One,* ed. Ruth Myers (New York: Church Publishing Incorporated, 1994) The phrase "baptismal paradigm" comes from Paul Avis as quoted in the essay, p. 4.

7 These thoughts are inspired by Paul Teitjen from "On Taking One's Daily Dip in the Baptismal Font: Baptismal Piety" in *Christian Initiation: Reborn of Water and Spirit,* ed. Daniel Brockopp, Brian Helgel, David Truemper (Valpariaiso, IN: Institute of Liturgical Studies, 1981), pp. 99 ff.

- **Baptismal Preparation and Practice:** Religious education, too, must be baptismally focused. It should not only inform but also form and transform people to live in right relationship with God and each other.[8] To do so requires that we "know about" our faith. A baptismal way of life would impel us to do better with baptismal preparation and practice. Just as musicians learn their music through constant rehearsing, so too must we practice our faith every day. Water by grace may bring us into the body of Christ, but it is knowledge that will enrich our understanding, and enlightened experience that will lead to growth that changes lives.[9] Two old and seemingly contradictory phrases capture the dialectic: "Christians are made, not born"; and "Faith is caught, not taught."

- **Baptismal Praxis and Pedagogy:** The context of how we teach is as important as the content. A baptismal praxis and pedagogy would help us nurture a deeper "knowing." Because we are walking on holy ground, it is necessary to offer education that is marked as distinctively religious. How we attend to formation and nurture cannot be at cross-purposes with who is being formed. In our educational efforts we must strive for more than the formal, school-based, teacher/learner model that has often existed to the exclusion of much less structured community storytelling, theological reflection, and contemplative use of the arts. Since we are trying to explain the unexplainable, facts aren't enough. Dealing with the numinous and mystical demands an imaginative expression. We need to leave room for more than words. We must also remember that "the church does not *have* an educational program, it *is* an educational program."[10] The local faith community teaches more by its actions than its words. Our worship, our social exclusions, our witness in the world (or lack of it) all speak volumes. We must pay attention not only to the explicit curriculum (actual courses of study) but the implicit (what is suggested by behavior and organization) and the null (what is taught by what is left out). The community must provide an environment in which all are profoundly educated and formed in faith, not merely well schooled.[11]

A Vision

What might such a baptismal ethos look like? This is not the place to detail all the possible manifestations, but mention of a few should illustrate and, it is hoped, inspire your imagination.[12]

Koinonia (The Curriculum of Community)
- There are joyful community celebrations of baptisms, and recognition of baptismal anniversaries, the same as is done for anniversaries of ordinations, marriages, and birthdays.

---

8 Thomas Groome, Sharing Faith: A Comprehensive Approach to Religious Education and Pastoral Ministry (New York: Harper Collins Publishers, 1991).

9 Thoughts here are inspired by Frederick Wolf's confirmation program, *Exploring Faith and Life*, along with various writings of William Willimon an Stanley Hauerwas.

10 Maria Harris, *Fashion Me a People* (Louisville: Westminster/John Knox Press, 1989), p.47.

11 For further reflections, see Maria Harris, *Teaching and Religious Imagination* (San Francisco: Harper and Row, 1987).

12 In the fashion of Maria Harris, the manifestations that follow are clustered in her five areas of curriculum of the church explained in *Fashion Me a People* pp.75 ff, chapters 4-8.

- There are frequent opportunities for people to share their life journeys and dilemmas, and regular times for the blessing of ministries and significant events (such as getting a driver's license or graduating from school).
- Prayers of the People actively involve all the assembled in the praying, as a proactive experience of corporate prayer.

Leiturgia (The Curriculum of Worship)
- Baptismal fonts (always filled with water) are up front and center in worship spaces, along with the paschal candle and altar, so that the water is encountered by all people at every time of worship.
- Rites of Initiation are given powerful, even dramatic, liturgical expression (vessels of water emptied noisily into font, liberal use of richly fragrant chrism, etc.); Holy Week, including a real Easter Vigil (i.e., with all the lessons, late at night or at dawn) is a central liturgical time in each community's yearly cycle.
- Worship is planned as a regular practice by liturgy committees comprised of community members along with the priest; worship is maximally participatory, takes advantage of all the senses, and provides many and varied opportunities for a direct experience of God.

Didache (The Curriculum of Teaching)
- Preparation for rites of initiation is planned with great care; learning in faith is presumed to be lifelong; there are abundant adult religious education programs that build a broad scriptural, sacramental, and Anglican literacy, and they are well attended.
- The home is seen as the "domestic church" and serves as the primary place of religious education, with expressions of faith regularly woven into family life.[13] For example: daily prayer is a part of life in a household; each home includes a dedicated place for worship; rituals are used to mark the "large" life passages as well as "small" ones.[14]
- Different learning styles and stages of faith development are taken into consideration in the planning and leading of worship and educational programs.
- Experiences of retreat and spiritual direction are commonplace events in the lives of all Christians.

---

13 There are many denominational resources and books to support faith development in the home. See Marjorie Thompson's concept of family as "domestic church" in her book *Family: The Forming Center* (Nashville: Upper Room Books, 1966).

14 One of the best ways for marking life passages in the home is with blessings: a house blessing when moving into a new home; anointing and blessing a child who is leaving home for college; prayers whenever a young person gets a driver's license, including a blessing of the car keys. See Nilsen Family, *For Everything A Season: 75 Blessings for Daily Life* (Des Moines, Iowa: Zion Publishing, 1999). In home rituals can take place upon the death or a pet or family member; by speaking the liturgical words of peace after an argument; in making the sign of the cross on a child's forehead before bed or when the child is leaving for school; using the Eucharistic words that begin the Great Thanksgiving as part of grace at meals followed by the sharing of gratitudes; gathering a circle of women family members to mark the beginning of menstruation of a daughter with the sharing words of wisdom; and of course the use of Advent wreaths and other seasonally appropriate rituals. See the series by Sharon Ely Pearson on *Faithful Celebrations*, and Ann Kitch's *Anglican Family Prayer Book*, both from Church Publishing.

Kerygma (The Curriculum of Proclamation)

- Every time a community of faith is gathered, someone tells a piece of the biblical story, and those gathered are invited to connect the story told to their lives.[15]
- Preaching actively engages the lives and hearts of the assembled, through frequent allusions to experiences of baptismal living, and messages that incorporate conversational moments and silent reflection.
- Sharing of faith with others is natural and not awkward for all Christians; people eagerly invite others to join them in worship; the question, "Whom are we excluding or missing?" is asked frequently.

Diakonia (The Curriculum of Service and Outreach)

- The tithe (giving 10%) becomes a minimum standard of giving for both churches (10% of their budgets to outreach) and individuals (10% of their time, talent, and treasure).
- There is a constant witness for justice and peace, locally and globally; as Jesus did, the community spends as much time with the marginalized people of the world as it does within the four walls of the church building.
- Prayers are worded in such a way as to call on God to give the assembly the wisdom and will to respond, rather than calling on God to be the celestial fixer of problems.
- Ecumenical and interfaith experiences are a regular part of church life.

Add your own dreams. If we strive for a baptismal paradigm and encourage baptismal piety, if we promote serious baptismal preparation and practice, and if we model elements of a baptismal praxis and pedagogy, these markers, and many others, will be made manifest.

Part Two: Content and Process

Water is an essential element of life, both biologically and spiritually. We are made of it and born out of it. A primal element that pre-exists earth's creation, water can symbolize both life and death. The world consists mostly of water. We cannot live long without it. We most notice the importance of water when it is not there. We drink water, and it quenches our thirst; we wash in it and become clean. Rain, snow, and ice give life to barren lands. When we are young (or young at heart), puddles give us endless joy. Water is a universal solvent that can clean everything but oil, and it douses threatening fires. We use waterways for travel.

Yet water's mysterious depths can drown someone or swamp any boat. In a storm or flood, it can wipe out all that comes before it. The power of water is uncontrollable. Any effort at containing water eventually erodes. Early civilizations could only comprehend this power by explaining that the sea was home to wild serpents. Not surprisingly, water is a fundamental

---

15 "Narrative Theology" is the term now used for the focus on the telling and weaving of biblical and life stories. See Tom Boomershine, *Story Journey* (Nashville: Abingdon Pres, 1988) and Herbert Anderson and Edward Foley *Mighty Stories, Dangerous Rituals: Weaving Together the Human and Divine* (San Francisco: Jossey-Bass, 1988).

religious symbol that permeates many cultures. Water appears often in scripture.[16] In baptisms, we thank God for the gift of water and recall a few of the stories: Creation, the Exodus from Egypt, and the Baptism of Christ.

As the title implies, water is the focusing metaphor for this book. The water image is explicitly used in Session One (in which we remember our baptisms) and returns in Session Eight (in which we contemplate living our baptisms). The image of water runs through all other sessions, appearing in each opening time of prayer and meditation, so that, by regularly and imaginatively encountering water, participants will feel washed and nourished.

The other six sessions are based on the vows of the Baptismal Covenant in the liturgy for Holy Baptism (see BCP, pp. 304–305). Session Two considers the three creedal questions relating to belief in the persons of the Trinity. Sessions Three through Seven focus on the other five baptismal vows. Since *Living Water* is grounded in the Episcopal tradition, the primary supplemental texts suggested for use are the Book of Common Prayer, our hymnals, and the Bible (NRSV translation). Often, when a congregation asks my help in finding a new curriculum, I remind them that their main resources are Prayer Books, Bibles, and hymnals. Those three resources are indispensable to catechesis. *Living Water* draws lightly upon many excellent sources, but the Prayer Book, Bible, and hymnals are this book's very well-springs.

Throughout the sessions, I rely loosely yet consistently on a process called "Shared Christian Praxis."[17] It is a free-flowing process, not a prescribed one. Try to keep the session movements fluid and prayerfully paced. Following is a summary of the process in *Living Water*. Included in the appendices you will find a generic lesson plan sheet that can be photocopied for planning purposes. It outlines the process and provides space for leaders' notes. There is also an appended "Session Materials" list.

Each session opens with a focusing time of prayer called "Gathering." The time of Gathering is followed by three more movements: one for storytelling, called "Sharing"; contemplation of scripture, other texts, and visual images, called "Reflecting"; and ways to practice the vows, called "Responding." Each session then closes in prayer. Plan to spend at least two hours on each session. Break each session into eight even blocks of time. Spend one block each on the opening and closing prayer time. Then give approximately two blocks each to the other three movements.[18]

---

16 A few passages to note: Water issues from Eden (Genesis 2). It kills and cleanses in the mythic story of Noah (Genesis 7 & 8). God gives Hagar a life-giving well in the desert (Genesis 21:19). In Isaiah and Psalms, there are abundant references to water as bringing life to the desert or cleansing the soul. There are references to living water (John 7:37-38, Revelation 22:1) and to pools of water as meeting places: Gibeon (2 Samuel 2:13); Mizpah (I Samuel 7:6); Hebron (2 Samuel 4:12); the pool of Samaria (I Kings 22:38); the upper pool on the highway to the Fuller's Field (Isaiah 7:3 and 36:2); and the lower pool (Isaiah 22:9-11). Bethesda and Siloam were pools where people went for healing (John 5:2-4; 9:7,11). The Samaritan woman meets Jesus at Jacob's well (John 4:1-39). Jesus teaches and feeds people by the sea (feeding of the 5,000 by the Sea of Galilee, and the post-resurrection appearance by the sea of Tiberias. And, of course, the baptism of Jesus.

17 Simply put, shared praxis is "a process of reflection on life and the wisdom of the ages in dialogue with others." For an in-depth presentation, see the previously cited book, *Sharing Faith*, by Thomas Groom. Especially note chapter 4 in which the movements of the process are described.

18 For example, if you have two hours: Use 15 min for the opening prayer; 30 min each for Sharing, Reflecting, and Responding; then another 15 min for closing prayer.

I. Gathering

This movement is a time to gather the group and contemplatively engage the theme of the session. It is a prayerful time that includes a simple song or chant, both a narrative passage of scripture and a poetic one from Psalms or Isaiah, a collect, and a version or adaptation of the Lords' Prayer. Rubric-like notes suggest creative ways in which the participants can engage themselves more fully in the scripture passages, prayers, and songs. Suggestions for a guided meditation on the scripture are offered. These are not for discussion, but rather for personal reflection. They are marked with a wave icon similar to the "waves" at the top of this page. You may chose to do this opening prayer within the context of "Daily Devotions for Individuals and Families" (BCP, p. 136ff).[19]

II. Sharing

At this point, participants are invited to share stories from life. A few stories from my own life and those of friends are included in the text, and are intended to prompt participants to recall similar experiences. Read one of these stories aloud expressively, or record it on a tape ahead of time to be played for the group. A creative sound engineer— if you know one—might be able to add appropriate background music and sounds. Suggestions are provided in the text that invite participants to share their own stories. These are boxed and marked with a wave icon. The sharing of stories works best by having the participants pair up or form sharing groups no larger than three, so that they will be telling their stories to one or two people, not to the entire group.

III. Reflecting

This movement has two parts. The first offers thematically chosen selections from scripture and Episcopal tradition (usually hymns and selections from the Prayer Book). There are two ways to use the suggested materials:

- Take time to read the passages ahead of time. Choose a few for your group to discuss as a whole. Do not try to deal with them all. Participants can reflect on the other passages outside of group time as they choose.
- Break into small groups and let each group choose one passage to study and discuss. Their discussion can then be summarized to the larger group.

A few brief comments on the chapter's theme are offered. You are invited to add additional content, but only in limited amounts. Remember that the emphasis needs to stay on discovery, not academic knowledge. What is encouraged is an inductive, not deductive, approach. Questions are provided that encourage reflection and conversation, again marked with a wave icon (cc). The aim is to place the personal stories of the participants into dialogue with God's Story.[20] For

---

19 Another tool for simple group prayer is *A Disciple's Prayer Book*. It is a pocket size version of the Daily Devotions that includes a brief time for scripture reflection. Available for free from the Episcopal Church, on-line at: https://www.episcopalchurch.org/wp-content/uploads/sites/2/2021/01/indigenous_disciples_prayer_book_eng.pdf

20 If you would like to spend more time is scripture reflection, see these two resources: In Dialogue with Scripture, Linda Grenz, ed. Available through Leader Resources http://www.leaderresources.org/assets/images/Youth/In_Dialogue_with_Scripture.pdf. Also see her concise and user-friendly resource by Linda Grenz, *Doubleday Pocket Bible Guide* (NY: Doubleday, 1997).

the second part of this movement, quotes, poems, and visual images are supplied for contemplation and discussion. Again, either choose a few suggestions for the attention of the entire group or let small groups choose a passage or two to consider.

IV. Responding

This movement is intended to lead the group to a faith response. Suggestions are provided for practicing what has been discovered. Half of the suggestions are intended for the group to consider together. A variety of styles of responses are provided: artistic responses, physical responses, ideas for discussion and journaling, and possible actions. Choose only one or two of the activities as appropriate to your group, or add your own ideas. Other suggestions are intended as personal exercises that participants may choose to undertake on their own.

Close each meeting in prayer with: 1) the song that was used in the time of Gathering; 2) free sharing of prayer needs; and 3) the baptismal prayer and dismissal that are provided in the text.

An option: If you have a limited time available for meetings, or if you would like to extend the process, you can divide the movements between two meetings. This pattern prevents the group time from becoming rushed, and allows participants a chance to sleep on what they have learned. The first meeting would contain Gathering, Sharing, and Reflecting. In the follow-up meeting, begin with the same Gathering prayer. For the rest of the follow-up, participants can: 1) share additional poems or quotes from the text, as well as other pieces they have discovered or written; 2) describe and discuss any personal insights or actions taken since the previous meeting; and 3) do the Responding activities. Close with prayer.

Audience

Since the life of faith is a community commitment, not just a private one, this resource is designed for group use. Ideally, the process should be held within the context of an ongoing community of faith, with the participants also being involved in parish life, worship, and outreach. With some adaptation, however, the material might serve as a guide for one-on-one spiritual direction or mentoring relationships. Similarly, individuals may be able to interpolate many aspects of this resource into private reflection and devotion.

It works best to limit a group to around 12 participants. Participants might include: 1) adults and youth preparing for baptism, confirmation, or reaffirmation of faith (although it is not intended as a complete program of preparation for confirmation/reception); and 2) parents and godparents of infants being baptized. But you need not limit participation to those in a process of initiation. Anyone will benefit from regular discernment about his or her faith and life. When using this process with those preparing for baptism, choose and adapt reflection questions accordingly. Although *Living Water* was written from and to the Episcopal Church in the United States, with thoughtful adjustments, it could be used anywhere within the Anglican Communion and also interdenominationally.

With some adaptation of the process, you will be able to gather intergenerational groups: children can bring the voice of creativity; youth, the voice of the prophet; adults, the voice of reason; and elders, the voice of wisdom. A study that includes all ages can be very rich, and allows the inclusion of families. If children are to be included, arrange for the full group to gather for opening and closing prayers. For Sharing, Reflecting, and Responding, offer parallel tracks for those under about age 12. When you regather as a large group for closing prayer, take some time to let the children share what they have learned.

Settings

Several settings work well for these sessions.

- *Living Water* can serve as a guide for a group retreat with the eight sessions being spread over a weekend. The weekend before Holy Week, Pentecost, or the feast of the Baptism of Our Lord Jesus Christ would be particularly appropriate.
- The sessions can be used as a seasonal study, with meetings held about once weekly through Lent/Easter (begin near the feast of the Baptism of Our Lord Jesus Christ and end at Easter or Pentecost) or Advent/Christmas (starting at All Saints' Day and ending in Epiphany at the Baptism of Our Lord).
- The sessions can be spaced out over a year. Two sessions on each of the Ember Days, or the days preceding baptismal dates encouraged in the Prayer Book (Easter Vigil, Pentecost, All Saints' Day, and the Baptism of Our Lord Jesus Christ) would work well.
- Portions of *Living Water* may be used as a follow-up to the Education for Ministry program (EFM); other portions may be integrated into the Journey to Adulthood program.

Creating Space

Great care should be given to the environment in which the group will meet. Parker Palmer suggests that "to teach is to create a space in which a community of truth can be practiced."[21] The environment and atmosphere that you set will proclaim the purpose of the gathering before a word is spoken. Here are some hints on how to create an environment in which imagination and creativity can flourish, and the Spirit can be heard.

- **Physical space:** Arrange the environment in which your group meets as intentionally as the altar guild sets the altar for Eucharist or a director sets a stage. Pay attention to lighting. Bright overhead light is harsh; lighting that is too dim can be aggravating. Lighting that is sufficient but indirect helps create a better space. The space should be as uncluttered as possible; less is definitely more in a space intended for a meditative process. The two most prominent features of the physical space are: 1) the arrangement of seats in a circle; and 2) the constant presence of a large, clear, glass bowl of water. Place it on a long, flowing scarf on the floor or on a low table in the center of the room (or use your imagination to highlight the bowl, perhaps with a spotlight, if you are lucky enough to be meeting in a place with adjustable lighting). This bowl of water is a

---

21 See Parker Palmer, *Courage to Teach* (San Francisco: Jossey Bass Publishers, 1998) p. 90 and pp. 73-77.

nonverbal witness to the symbolic importance of water in all sessions. Some reflection questions direct the participant's attention to the water, and provide ways of engaging it.

- **Hospitable Space:** The process used in *Living Water* is a contemplative one that includes a great deal of faith-sharing and life-sharing. This can be awkward for those who are used to a less personal, more academic, classroom-based environment. From the start, take care to create an atmosphere of trust. This is particularly important at the initial gathering. Allow ample time for introductions and group-building. Begin by asking participants to introduce themselves and share a general bit of information with an icebreaker question.[22]

  Be sure to clearly outline for the group the content, process, and expectations of these sessions. Let them know they can opt out of any exercise along the way. The discussion options in Session One are designed to help a new group get rolling. In subsequent sessions, begin each Sharing segment by inviting participants to share brief insights gained in their individual reflections since last meeting. You may like to provide everyone with a notebook they can use for some of the exercises, for journaling and storywriting, and for recording thoughts and questions during and between gatherings of the group.

  To help build as sense of safety and community, name and agree upon basic norms that will foster and honor everyone's participation. This includes being scrupulously inclusive (so that all have a chance to be heard), nurturing the art of deep listening with silence between speakers (perhaps using a talking stick) and the art of asking "honest, open questions."[23] Establish a high level of trust by discussing the importance of confidentiality. Regular attendance by all participants is an important demonstration of trust; participants will not feel honored by those who casually come and go.

- **Spiritual Space:** Each session begins and ends with a time of prayer. The opening prayer—the Gathering—helps the group enter the theme contemplatively. End meetings in a similarly prayerful fashion. Prayers and suggestions are provided for this purpose at the end of each session. Do not rush the times of prayer, and allow for silent moments between spoken or sung words. It is in quiet moments that the Spirit and the "inner voice" speak to us. Throughout the process allow for quiet times as needed for reflection (this is especially important for those who have a quieter or more introverted personality). There are many other ways to mark space and time as holy: place a candle or two in the midst of the group to be lit as you begin each session and extinguished ceremonially at the end; or ring a bell or gong at the beginning and end of gatherings.

---

22 A simple icebreaker is to pair up the participants and have them interview each other until they find ten things they hold in common. Pairs then share their results with the group. For other icebreaker ideas, ask your youth ministers, they always have games up their sleeves.

23 The good list of guidelines for faith-based groups comes from the former organization "Faith at Work" (see appended, p.212). Also helpful are the "Touchstones" for Circles of Trust, from Parker Palmer's work with "The Center for Courage and Renewal" available for download at www.couragerenewal.org/wpccr/touchstones/. For reflections on the art of listening and asking questions see Palmer's book, *Hidden Wholeness* (San Francisco: Jossey Bass, 2004), especially chapters 7 and 8. Urban Confessional promotes "free listening" on the street. Wonderful videos on the power of listening and how to be a good listener, are available on their website at www.urbanconfessional.org/. See also the book *Short Paragraphs on Listening* by their founder, Benjamin Mathes.

- **Artistic Space:** St. Augustine is known to have said that those who sing pray twice! Have thematically appropriate music playing as people enter. A simple opening song or chant is provided for each session of *Living Water*. Singing it at the beginning and the end of each meeting will place the theme in the soul in a profound way. For easy access, most music suggested in the sessions comes primarily from Episcopal hymnals (*Wonder, Love, and Praise; Lift Every Voice and Sing II*; and *The Hymnal 1982*).[24] Feel free to expand beyond these sources into musical traditions familiar to you and the culture of your group. If you are a session leader who is not musically inclined, and who is hesitant to lead group singing, invite someone who can be a music leader to become part of the group. You can also bring in recordings of the suggested songs. Use commercial recordings or, if someone in your parish is handy with instruments and recording equipment, make your own. With a bit of advance warning, your church choir director or organist may be able to create a tape for you that includes all the songs you will need.

  Be sure to use the other arts. Take to heart the old proverb "A picture speaks a thousand words" and incorporate visual art into your process. The artists among us are often prophets who can express the inexpressible. You might place an icon of the baptism of Christ, photographs of baptisms, or other images in the room as a way to illustrate and elucidate specific session themes.[25] Poets, too, are prophetic. Their nondiscursive communication is especially needed when encountering the mysteries of faith. Some poems are included in the Reflecting movement. Feel free to bring other poems to the sessions. Consider expanding or extending the process even further by viewing films together, or read books on the themes of each session and then discuss them.

Invite participants to help you create the space and contribute creatively to the content of each session. Encourage group members to look ahead at session themes and bring appropriate symbols, images, poems, or recorded music to enrich meetings. They can be asked to lead times of prayer. Ask everyone to arrive a few minutes early and to enter the space quietly to allow for a time of personal meditation. Similarly, urge participants to avoid disbanding in a chatty fashion, but rather to take additional personal time for reflection and then to slip out quietly. This kind of attention to the environment and nurture of the group must be carefully encouraged in the beginning, but, when attended to, a group ownership of the process takes over. The result is that everyone participates in creating a sacred space that allows for prayerful conversation and exploration of faith.

---

24 A few hymns come from *The New Century Hymnal*, published by The Pilgrim Press of the United Church of Christ; and the Roman Catholic hymnal *Gather* which is available via GIA Publications. Both hymnals are worth obtaining for their rich selection of hymns.

25 A rich resource for art images, is *Imaging the Word*, from United Church Press, one volume for each of the cycles of the common lectionary. In addition to poetry and other quotes, each volume contains color reproductions of artwork that relates to one of the appointed lessons for the day. It is now out of print, but finding a used set through Amazon, is worth it. Another ready source for visual art images is to search scripture passages in Google Images.

Other Possibilities

• Encourage participants to spend additional time reflecting on each topic between sessions. A rhythm of group and individual time is helpful, as are other rhythms of speech and silence, prayer and study, conversation and listening, story and reflection.

• Invite each participant to find a spiritual companion for the journey. The two can covenant to meet regularly for discussion, sharing, discernment, prayer, or service. Ideally, the pairs should attend the group circle time together. (If the partner is not a member of the group, the participant must be careful to maintain the group's confidentiality.)

A Final Comment

As you use *Living Water,* please keep in mind that this is not an educational "program." Rather it is a formational "process" that is intuitive, and is intended to be used flexibly. There are other books that teach about baptism in a more didactic way, and you may choose to use them as follow-up studies. However, for this process, group leaders should not attempt to lead as an instructor would lead students through a structured curriculum; rather, they must undergo the contemplative experience of exploration and discovery right along with the other participants. Each person, each group has a distinctive culture and distinctive needs. All those who use this guide should adapt and expand upon it. The collection of stories, biblical passages, hymns, prayers, quotes, and poems that are offered come only from my personal experiences of leading such a process in a variety of settings, and from the contributions of friends and colleagues. The suggestions are just that—suggestions; and they are far from exhaustive. This book is only a starting point. Freely add your own music, words, and images as best suits the culture and needs of your group. Generally, consider this a work in progress to which you contribute.

I now invite you to the water's edge where mysteries, miracles, and visions—perhaps even the dancing of the loons—await. As you continue to return to the "living water," may you come to know more of "living the water" of baptism. Go to the water reflectively and meditatively. Return often. You may choose to just look. You might drink. Perhaps you will wade or swim. Maybe you will want to wash. The goal of this resource is simply to lead you there, and help you lead others, so that together we immerse ourselves. It is no trifling matter. It is your very life.

July 4

I have been here three days, but have not seen the loons.
We hear them at night, so they are here somewhere.
In the kayak this morning, went to the cove on the island
to look for the nest. It is not in the regular place!
Where are they? Usually we see a chick by the 4th of July.
Maybe they are still nesting, or just staying out of the way
this holiday weekend. It has been raining a lot.
The lake is high. I hope the nests aren't flooded again.

Session One

Remember your baptism, and be thankful!

Gathering

Place small clear glass nuggets, the kind used in flower arranging, in a large bowl of water in the center of the group. There should be more nuggets than there are participants.

OPENING SONG: ## Shall We Gather at the River

This is a classic baptismal hymn, found in Lift Every Voice and Sing II, #141. *A beautiful setting of the hymn is on the recording* God Help Us *by the Miserable Offenders (see appendix). "Take Me to the Water" from* Lift Every Voice and Sing II #134 *is another appropriate hymn, or "Down in the River to Pray." which is available on the soundtrack of the film,* O Brother, Where Art Thou?

Shall we gather at the river,
Where bright angel feet have trod;
With its crystal tide forever
Flowing by the throne of God?

On the margin of the river,
Washing up its silver spray,
We will walk and worship ever,
All the happy golden day.

Ere we reach the shining river,
Lay we ev'ry burden down;
Grace our spirits will deliver,
And provide a robe and crown.

Soon we'll reach the shining river,
Soon our pilgrimage will cease,
Soon our happy hearts will quiver
With the melody of peace.

> *Refrain:*
> Yes, we'll gather at the river,
> The beautiful, the beautiful river;
> Gather with the saints at the river
> That flows by the throne of God.

MARK 1:9–11   The Baptism of Christ

Read the following passage aloud. Leave a moment of silence, then read it a second time.

*The second reading can be from the parallel passage in Matthew 3:13–17,
or from a paraphrase such as* The Message *by Eugene H. Peterson.*

In those days Jesus came from Nazareth of Galilee
    and was baptized in the Jordan by John.
And just as he was coming up out of the water,
he saw the heavens torn apart
    and the Spirit descending like a dove on him.
And a voice came from heaven,
    "You are my Son, the Beloved;
        with you I am well pleased."

ISAIAH 40:3–5

Proclaim this in unison.

A voice cries out:
    "In the wilderness prepare the way of the LORD,
    make straight in the desert a highway for our God.
    Every valley shall be lifted up,
        and every mountain and hill be made low
    the uneven ground shall become level,
        and the rough places a plain.
    Then the glory of the LORD shall be revealed,
        and all people shall see it together,
        for the mouth of the LORD has spoken."

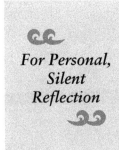

For Personal, Silent Reflection

Spend a few moments in silence trying to imagine what Jesus may have been experiencing as he was immersed in God at his baptism.

What was "torn open" for Jesus? What emotions were sparked?

How was Jesus different after the event?

What were his questions after the experience?

What is it like to live with the word "beloved" coming from God, while being in touch with the reality of your whole self and life?

Remember a time when you felt God's blessing in a remarkable way.

The Lord's Prayer

Our Father, who art in heaven,
    hallowed be thy Name,
    thy kingdom come,
    thy will be done,
        on earth as it is in heaven.
Give us this day our daily bread.
And forgive us our trespasses,
    as we forgive those
    who trespass against us.
And lead us not into temptation,
    but deliver us from evil.
For thine is the kingdom,
    and the power, and the glory,
    for ever and ever. Amen.

Collect

Father in heaven,
who at the baptism of Jesus in the River Jordan,
proclaimed him your beloved Son
and anointed him with the Holy Spirit:
Grant that all who are baptized into his Name
may keep the covenant they have made,
and boldly confess him as Lord and Savior;
who with you and the Holy Spirit lives and reigns,
One God, in glory everlasting. Amen.

> — The Baptism of our Lord Jesus Christ,
> The Book of Common Prayer, p. 214

Sharing

UNFORTUNATELY I DO NOT remember my baptism. I was only about six months old when it happened in a Presbyterian Church in Roanoke, Virginia. It was only a few years ago that I even learned of the date, June 5, after finding my baptismal certificate in a scrapbook of memories Mom had kept for me.

The service did not take place in my family's church (we lived in Ohio at the time and were in Virginia to visit relatives). My parents were given no formal preparation for my baptism, other than some practice of the order of service. They did not even know the pastor or the congregation. But my infant cousin Ginny—one of the relatives we visited—also needed baptizing, and my parents and Ginny's parents wanted us to be baptized together. Her parents would be my godparents. The strong faith of my mother and aunt grounded Ginny's and my baptism. It was a faith that miraculously pulled Mom's family through the siege of Budapest during World War II. Their experiences are chronicled in my aunt's adolescent diary. It is a story of death and resurrection. The saga begins with their fleeing to Budapest, just before Christmas Eve, 1944. For eight weeks, they survived terror and near starvation, and returned home just before the following Easter Sunday. Not much later, with politics changing for the worse, and little hope for the future, they emigrated to the United States to start over.

Our baptisms were no small thing for the family. We cousins were a sign that the family would continue, after the trauma of war. Ginny and I, along with another cousin, Emeric, were the first members of my mother's family to be born in this country. Emeric was named after two men in a long family line of Hungarian Reformed Church clergy: our great-uncle who was a heroic bishop during the beginning of the Communist takeover of Hungary, and a great-great-grandfather who had been a renowned pastor, theology professor, and statesman. My name, Klara, goes back three generations in the same family line. I wear a ring that belonged to the Klaras before me.

Although I can't recall my baptism, there is a Hungarian custom that has served to remind me of who I am and whose I am. Each day on the calendar has a saint's name associated with it, and all those who are named after that saint take the day as a Name Day. On their Name Days, they are greeted with kisses on both cheeks, celebrated with flowers and cards, and held in prayer. My name day is August 12. In our family, the occasion is noted at the dinner table with a ring of flowers circling the family member's plate. To this day, my mother, my godmother/aunt, and Aunt Klara in Hungary send me a Name Day card. If I am home, the flowers still ring my place at the table.

Desert Baptism, When I Was Seven

— by Gary Barker

I recall the green hose penetrating the space between white fence boards
Pouring clear, cool liquid in my hand-dug lake,
A little hole not even eight inches deep secreted behind the garage.
This thirsty bit of Southern California soaked up the offering;
It disappeared with only a hint of dark wet where it entered the desert.

Extravagantly, I stood in my dusty swim trunks,
    Hose at my hip,
    Like a Greek god in miniature,
    Waiting.
What would Mom say if she found out,
    If she heard the scream of the water in the pipes?
I knew.
Still, I watched the precious sunlight fall into the ground.

The gravel boiled, slowly at first, but then like a flood;
As if the life swallowed into the ground was suddenly birthed up.

The faucet off,
The telltale hose returned through the fence,
I sat down by my lake.
I reached into my bulging pocket to find a toy boat
And placed it on the new surface—where cloud and sun and cerulean blue rippled
    Together—to float.

Emergence

— by Jenny St. Julien

I COUNTED my pregnancy with Jake in moons instead of months. For ten lunar cycles I carried this babe in the waters of my womb. Jake's emergence was such a blessed and pure event. My fantasy of a "perfect birth" experience was to give birth at home, attended only by family and friends. I didn't dare to plan such a thing, but that is how his birth came to pass.

One hot summer night, and on his due date, I was awakened by the sounds of gunshots in the distance. I pulled my husband close for comfort, and we joined our bodies in lovemaking. Shortly after, the waters portending Jacob's arrival appeared. Things progressed, and I was quickly in the transitional phase of labor. When I spoke to my midwife on the phone, my voice felt as if it were coming from the depths of my being. Grunting and groaning, I asked, "Does it sound like I can make it to the hospital?" I didn't want to wind up delivering my baby onto the floor of my car. I was sure that she could tell by my voice that my baby would be born soon.

Although there were some pains with my labor, I've never felt more at peace than I did in those moments. Jessica, my daughter, was so gleeful as she skipped up the street to my friend Deanne's house to get a bulb syringe for suctioning the baby's nose. When my two best friends arrived and came into my bedroom, I looked into their fearful faces and told them, "Everything is fine; calm down. I'm having my baby here on my bed." I had prepared a prayer for the transitional phase, and prayed with each contraction, "Thank you, God. This contraction brings my baby another step closer to me." It was a quick birth, but it passed as if in slow motion for me.

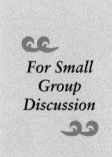

For Small Group Discussion

Reach into the bowl of water and take a glass bead. Imagine that it is a drop of water. Hold it as you recall a memory of baptism, your own or someone else's. Think both literally and figuratively.

Share your stories and feelings about the event with another person in the circle.
For those with no experience of baptism, consider a time of beginning something new and fresh that made a big difference in your life.

Share stories of birth—either of giving birth to a child, or watching a birth, or telling what you know of your own birth.
Is there a time when you have figuratively given birth to something in your life?
A time when you midwifed new life in another person?

Read the genealogy of Christ in the first chapter of Matthew.
How did you come to be named? How did you come to name your children?

I felt a guiding clarity, a trust in the birth process that felt stronger than any trust I had ever felt before. I knew that my baby and I would be safe, that the desire I had for him to be born at home was becoming a reality. I was blessed to be the first one to touch Jacob's wet, hairy head as it crowned, and later to pull his soft fleshiness from my body by my own hands. Laying him on my belly, I waited for a minute or so, before picking him up to determine his gender, and, as in a dream I had had some time ago, he was a boy. In that dream he had written words on my socks: "LOVE" on my left foot's sock, "JACOB" on my right foot's sock. My husband, my daughter, my son Jeremy, and my two friends encircled me and Jacob, and I picked him up and said, "Welcome to the world, Jacob!" It was a peaceful and easy journey that filled us all to overflowing with a divine Joy. We had been visited by God's presence on that day, Jacob's emergence day. In pictures taken just after his birth, the joy is apparent in our glowing faces. For me, it was a baptism of spirit; a threshold had been crossed. I felt some fear, but allowed that fear to be quickly washed away by the trust I felt in God and in the ability of my own body to do what it knows to do, without me or anyone else getting in its way.

The Chinese character for "water" evolved from a symbol showing the main flow of a river with eddies swirling from the sides. Like other symbols in Chinese, the image has become stylized.

You might try tracing the strokes as a meditation. Draw the downward central stroke first, then the left eddy, then the right eddy.

In Session Eight, you will find the Chinese word for "eternity," which has the same strokes with the addition of a spot of ink above the main flow of the river, representing a complex concept of "foreverness" as a flow that never ends.

Reflecting

Scripture

Genesis 1:1–8	First two days of creation
Exodus 2:1–10	Birth of Moses
Mark 10:35–45	James and John, sons of Zebedee, come to question Jesus
Luke 2:21–30	Jesus named and presented in the temple
John 3:1–8	Nicodemus questions Jesus about being born again of the Spirit
Acts 2:37–47	Pentecost
Acts 8:9–24	Philip in Samaria
Acts 9:1–19	The conversion of Saul
(also Acts 22:6–16; 26:12–18)	
Acts 10	Baptism of Cornelius and the Gentiles
Romans 6:3–11	Dying and rising with Christ
Romans 8:11–17	Life in the Spirit
Galatians 3:23–29	All are one in Christ
Ephesians 4:1–6	Unity in Christ

For Small and Large Group Discussion

Refer to the scripture selections. Choose one or two that speak to you, and discuss them.

What word or phrase jumps out at you?

What does the passage say to you?

What is it calling you to do?

Consider any of the suggested hymns that relate to your conversation. Read over the Prayer Book selections and comments.

What light do they shed on your conversation?

Hymns

The Hymnal 1982
> The sinless one to Jordan came, #120
> When Jesus went to Jordan's stream, #139

Lift Every Voice and Sing II
> Deep river, #8
> Hush, hush, #128
> Take me to the water, #134
> Shall we gather at the river, #41

Wonder, Love, and Praise
> Baptized in water, #767

The Book of Common Prayer

The Catechism, p. 858
> What is Holy Baptism?
> What is the outward and visible sign
> in Baptism?
> What is the inward and spiritual grace
> in Baptism?

A Thanksgiving for the Birth or
> Adoption of a Child, pp. 439–445

Thanksgiving over the Water, p. 306

> *(Also look at similar prayers in liturgies of
> other denominations. A collection can be found
> in* Liturgy, *vol. 15, no. 3.)*

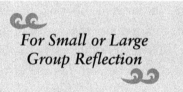

*For Small or Large
Group Reflection*

Return to the baptismal moment that
you shared.

> What did you take into the water
> that died there?

> What came to life?

> What was made clean?

> What led you there?

> What changed for you?

> How do you feel about the Christian
> focus upon images of death as a way
> toward life?

Describe a moment of conversion, a time
of transformation when your heart and
mind were changed.

> Has baptism made a difference in your life?

> What difference might it make?

The Greeks had a verb for immerse which was "baptizo," one for sprinkle that was "rantizo," and one for pour that was "cheo." Of these, it was the one that suggests the most bodily interaction with water that became the root of the scriptural word for what we know as baptism. Implied is a total immersion. In presentations he makes on adult faith and baptism, Micki Corso goes even further when he puts it this way: "Baptism is not a ritual bathing; it is a ritual drowning! In early baptisms, after being held under the water three lengthy times, you came up gasping for breath. You knew you had died. Why was it that people such as St. Francis could work with lepers, and Mother Theresa with the lowest outcasts? It didn't matter because they were dead already! They simply had nothing to fear."

Luther said that the Christian life was nothing less than a daily baptism. Just as in any committed relationship, our relationship with God as marked in baptism, has profound and practical implications that must be lived and worked out every day.

A Methodist scholar, Lawrence Stookey has been known to shout a joyous appeal to his students as he runs across his campus in the rain: "Remember your baptism, and be thankful!" Paul Teitjen, in an essay, "Taking a Daily Dip in the Baptismal Font," suggests that we be "robin-like" in our remembering, that we find ways to dip our hearts and minds daily into the baptismal font in a manner that will call us to "ongoing dying and rebirth, repentance and renewal."

There are other ways to remember one's baptism. Perhaps we should all put a sign in our shower telling us to remember our baptism so that while immersed in the cleansing water each day, we would give thanks. Or what if we placed a bowl of water near the front door? Upon seeing it when leaving home and entering the world, it would remind us of our baptism. In returning, it might invite us to examine how we lived the day. When an extra reminder is needed, or to seal the day's end and bless the coming sleep, we could dip fingers in that bowl of holy water and make the sign of the cross. In my bowl of water are colorful rocks that have been collected from memorable places.

A Methodist scholar, Lawrence Stookey, has once or twice been heard shouting a joyous appeal to his students as he runs across his campus in the rain: "Remember your baptism, and be thankful!" Perhaps we should all put a sign in our shower telling us to remember our baptism. As we are immersed in the cleansing water each day, we would give thanks.

Reflectively read one or two of the following quotes. What is your response?

While God might have driven Adam and Eve out of the Garden of Paradise, God still ensured that the living waters issuing from the garden continued to irrigate the whole earth and cleanse its polluted streams and lakes. When we bless water, we acknowledge God's grace and desire to cleanse the world and make it paradise.

Water is the blood of creation. Our own bodies are eighty percent water. Water is also the element of baptism. St. Thomas Aquinas said: "Because water is transparent, it can receive light; and so it is fitting that it should be used in baptism, inasmuch as it is the sacrament of faith." By cleansing the water we make it clear again. By expelling the demonic pollutants we ready it for greater service to God. We tend not only the garden that we call nature but also the garden that is ourselves, insofar as we are constituted of water and are born anew by it.

— Vigen Guroian, *Inheriting Paradise: Meditations on Gardening*, p. 9

You don't miss your water till the well runs dry.

— an old saying

Water to me is a saving grace. As a child I forgot my anger at my parents or camp counselors or teachers if I went to a swimming pool, or to a lake.... Water was freedom, an element in which I believed I had perfect control. Lake and pool waters were calm enough to provide that illusion. I moved through the water in a kind of ecstasy, cut away from the rules of the land, social requirements, limitations, disapproval. Water was action, more effective than prayer. When I swam I believed in God.

— Doris Grumbach, *Coming into the End Zone: A Memoir*

What do I do now?

I listen to water

  Falling

    Into

the

    Gentleness

      Of being

Nothing

  More

    Than liquid sound.

And I, at last,

  Want nothing

    More.

— W. Paul Jones, *A Table in the Desert: Making Space Holy*

If the church is truly Christ's body, then it must participate in his *baptisma*; it must continue to share in the death and resurrection experience through which humankind encounters salvation. The ecclesial sign of sustained participation in Christ's *baptisma* is the baptism through which every Christian enters the grace-ful mystery of redemption. It is the life-saving, life-changing nature of baptism that makes it the fundamental sacrament of the Christian community. Without it the church does not exist. When it is devalued, discounted, put off to the side, the church is essentially weak. When baptism is seen as utterly basic and central, the church comes to life....
[P]arishes with a high doctrine of baptism and a vigorous approach to the process of initiation will be vital centers of Christian life and witness.

— A. Theodore Eastman, *The Baptizing Community*, pp. 31, 36

Bathe yourself in the ocean of matter; plunge into where it is deepest and most violent; struggle in its currents and drink of its waters. For it cradled you long ago in your pre-conscious existence; and it is that ocean that will raise you up to God.

— Pierre Teilhard de Chardin, as quoted in *A Sourcebook about Liturgy*, Liturgy Training Publications, p. 136

Baptism

If I could tell you what this meant,
this threefold phrase, this fluid touch,
this moment sanctified by promise,
you in your infant distraction
would certainly dismiss it,
and I, the priest who dried your head
then lit a candle for remembrance,
might realize again some things are taught
but others are best lived and learned
as is most discernment.
Still, something happened on this day
of such great simplicity,
it might pass by unrecognized.
Clearly there was not birth and death
with human severance and pain.
But portals opened that are unseen
and forces moved to befriend your soul.
You were enrolled into God.
This may seem a small thing
in the surety of youth
but trust as those who brought you here:
There is nothing more.

— Penelope Duckworth,
The Christian Century, February 7–14, 1996

Baptism announces that water is thicker than blood....
Insisting that baptism is only and essentially a family affair transforms this dangerous ritual into a tame, domestic event.

— Herbert Anderson and Edward Foley, *Mighty Stories, Dangerous Rituals,* p. 65

Whenever water appears [in dreams or visions] it is usually the water of life, meaning a medium through which one is reborn. It symbolizes a sort of baptism ceremony, or initiation, a healing bath that gives resurrection or rebirth.

The baptismal font is the return to the womb of consciousness, since consciousness has arisen in that state. The return to such a condition has healing value, because it brings things back to their origin, where nothing is disturbed, yet everything is still right. It is as if one were gaining there a sort of orientation of how things really ought to be.

— C. G. Jung, as quoted in *An Easter Sourcebook,* Liturgy Training Publications, p. 137

On Easter Monday we have gone to an early Mass to hear the delightful gospel and the Alleluias again. Then we have always found a body of water to visit and enjoy—a river, a lake, a stream, the marshes—fresh, life-giving waters like that which was blessed in the Vigil service, like the waters of our baptism which we remember at this time. The story of Emmaus seems to inspire a walk in nature. We see the evidence of transformation all around us in the new green of springtime....

Always we got wet. We learned about the traditions of getting wet on Easter Monday first from a favorite children's book which we have read and reread for years, especially at Eastertime. *The Good Master* by Kate Seredy tells of a Hungarian family, and the accounts of their Easter celebrations especially caught our interest. On Easter Monday, the young boys of the Hungarian villages went from house to house, and wherever young girls lived, they came up to the door, recited a blessing and then splashed the girls with water. The girls in turn invited them in and everyone feasted on Easter specialties, and the girls gave the boys some of their carefully painted eggs to take home. On Easter Tuesday they replayed the whole game in reverse.

Then a Polish friend of mine surprised me one Easter Monday morning with such a wet blessing, and "it took." Our children felt so inspired that it has become a part of our Easter Monday rites at the water's edge.

— Gertrud Mueller Nelson, *To Dance with God*, pp. 184–185

I undressed, dove into the sea, and swam. I felt the sacrament of baptism in all its deathless simplicity on that day, understood why so many religions consider water and the bath, in other words baptism, the indispensable, presupposed condition of initiation before a convert begins new life. The water's coolness penetrates to the marrow of the bones, to the very pith; it finds the soul, and thus, seeing the water, beats its wings happily like a young sea gull, washes itself, rejoices, and is refreshed. The simple everyday water is transubstantiated; it becomes the water of eternal life and renews the person. When the convert emerges from the water, the world seems changed. The world has not changed, it is always wonderful and horrible, iniquitous and filled with beauty. But now, after baptism, the eyes that see the world have changed.

— Nikos Kazantzakis, as quoted in *A Sourcebook about Liturgy*, Liturgy Training Publications, p. 3

Water is always an invitation to immersion [for me], an immersion with a quality of totality, since it would accept all of me, as I am. Some primal urge invites me to return whence I came.

At times I have done so. There is some special delight in simply walking into a stream, stepping into a lake. The child's delight in a puddle is my adult's in the sea....

No rain falls that I do not at once hear in the sound of the falling water an invitation to come to the wedding. It is rare that I do not answer. A walk in an evening rain in any setting is to walk in the midst of God's loving attention to his earth, and, like a baptism, is no simple washing, but a communication of life. When you hurry in out of the rain, I hurry out into it, for it is a sign that all is well, that God loves, that good is to follow. If suffering a doubt, I find myself looking to rain as a good omen. And in rain, I always hear singing, wordless chant rising and falling.

When rain turns to ice and snow I declare a holiday. I could as easily resist as stay at a desk with a parade going by in the street below. I cannot hide the delight that then possesses my heart. Only God could have surprised rain with such a change of dress as ice and snow....

Most people love rain, water. Snow charms all young hearts. Only when you get older and bones begin to feel dampness, when snow becomes a traffic problem and a burden in the driveway, when wet means dirt—then the poetry takes flight and God's love play is not noted.

But I am still a child and have no desire to take on the ways of death. I shall continue to heed water's invitation, the call of the rain. We are in love and lovers are a little mad.

> — Matthew Kelty, *Flute Solo: Reflections of a Trappist Hermit*,
> pp. 117–119, as cited in *Space for God* by Don Postema, p. 66

Creature of Water

I bless thee, creature of water, through God the Living, through God the Holy, who in the beginning by his word did separate thee from the dry land and did command thee to water the earth in four streams, who in the desert gave a sweetness to thy bitterness, that all might drink thee, and for a thirsty people did bring thee forth from a rock.

I bless thee through Jesus Christ his only son our Lord, who by his power in a wonderful sign at Cana of Galilee did change thee into wine, who walked upon thee with his feet, who was baptized by John in Jordan, who did shed thee from his side mingled with blood, and commanded his disciples to baptize believers.

> — an ancient Gallican-Celtic prayer, from *Liturgy*, vol. 15, no. 3

Refreshment

Floating in a pond on a hot summer's day
Your sunlight radiating within and without me
Bathing me in the warmth of your goodness.
Bullfrogs croaking
Dragonflies mating
Birds singing
Fish jumping
A splash of cool water—
            Ahhh...
"Come to me all ye that travail
    and are heavy-laden
    and I will refresh you."
            — Elizabeth Rankin Geitz,
                Women's Uncommon Prayers, p. 238

Christ Impatient

"You waters of
my christening,
you're no
summer pond:
come,
drink me down!"
            — Pete Green (unpublished)

Of Birthing

Human birth,
pain, messy, sticky, sweaty,
push—breathe, push—breathe,
no pain, no gain,
push—breathe, push—breathe,
finally, new life.

Spiritual birth,
what does this mean?
pain, struggle, water, sweat,
no pain, no gain.
Trust in God.

I push against my own will.
God breathes new life into me,
push—breathe, push—breathe.

Wind and water.
No, I don't want to go,
the wind blows,
God's breath surrounds me.
I resist
push—breathe, push—breathe.
The water of baptism engulfs me.
I am made new.

Human birth, spiritual birth.
I don't remember the first.
I don't remember the second either.
It happened gradually—a long litany of
push—breathe, push—breathe,
not willing to fully give myself over to God.
            — Marjorie A. Burke,
                Women's Uncommon Prayers, p. 128

Responding

Practicing Together:

- A font is a container that holds baptismal water. Look at pictures of fonts throughout history. It is interesting to note that, as our awareness of baptism became smaller, so did our fonts, our preparation for initiation, and our baptismal rituals. What impact has the diminished theology had on our understanding of lived faith?

- Go into your sanctuary. Walk around and feel the space. What does it say to you? Notice where the font is placed and what it is like. Does it have water in it? What does that say about your theology of baptism? When and how is baptism celebrated in your community? Describe it. What does your ritual symbolize? Does it express what your community believes? If not, what might be changed?

- What difference has baptism made in the life of your community? What difference might it make?

- Using watercolors and special watercolor paper, create some free-flowing representations of water. It could be a single, large watercolor done by the group together, or individual renderings. If you have artists in your midst, ask them to share suggestions on technique. Have sounds of water, or music that evokes water, playing in the background.

Practicing at Home:

- Do you know the date of your baptism? If yes, how do or might you celebrate it, individually and with others? If you do not know when you were baptized, try to find the date and as much as you can about the circumstances. Who were your godparents? Write a letter to them, or to the clergy person who baptized you, and tell them about your faith journey.

- If you are preparing to be baptized, think about when you would like it to happen. Who would you like to be there? Is there a song you might like to have sung, or a particular prayer said? Who will be your sponsor or godparents? Once you have a sponsor or godparents, spend time with them, learn about their faith journey and share your own.

- Meditate on the place of water in your life, and on its power for creation and destruction. What insights have you experienced during a renewing spring shower, or a violent storm, or a day fishing in a stream? Write down any truths that God has shown you through the gift of water.

— adapted from *The Christian Formation Bible*, p. 9

- What would be the nearest natural source of water for your home if modern systems were to fail? Enjoy the gift of water, and give thanks for it.

— adapted from *The Christian Formation Bible*, p. 354

- Water is the main element in creation stories of most cultures around the world. Go to a library, find and read a variety of indigenous creation stories. Reflect on them. What common themes do you find?

- There is a wealth of children's books that are retellings of the Genesis creation story. If you have children, go to a library and find creation stories for children. Read them aloud with your children, and talk about them.

Closing Prayer

Sing again the song, "Shall we gather at the river," which was sung in the time of Gathering.
Take a moment to share thanksgivings and personal prayer needs.
Close with the following prayer and blessing.

Heavenly Father, we thank you that by water and the Holy Spirit you have bestowed upon us your servants the forgiveness of sin, and have raised us to the new life of grace. Sustain us, O Lord, in your Holy Spirit. Give us inquiring and discerning hearts, the courage to will and to persevere, a spirit to know and to love you, and the gift of joy and wonder in all your works. Amen.

— The Book of Common Prayer, p. 308 (adapted)

May God, who sent the Holy Spirit to rest upon the Only-begotten at his baptism in the Jordan River, pour out that Spirit on us who have come to the waters of new birth. Amen.

— Season Blessings, Epiphany,
The Book of Occasional Services (adapted)

Upon leaving, reach into the bowl of water in the center of the room, and take out some small glass beads. Place them in a bowl of water at home. Put the bowl in a place you will encounter daily, perhaps by a door. Let that place become an altar for you. Regularly touch the water and remember baptismal moments.

July 18

I found our nest! It is on the leeward side of a tiny island on the other side of the lake, by a marshy, undeveloped area. I was out in the kayak going around the shore. Just around a bend, was surprised by the sight of the nest with the loon on it, right in front of me! The loon had her neck pulled down level with the ground, hiding behind the grasses. I wish I had remembered to take a camera! It is late to be nesting. Guess it's a second try this year.

Session Two

Do you believe in God the Father?
Do you believe in Jesus Christ, the Son of God?
Do you believe in God the Holy Spirit?

Gathering

Arrange a collection of crosses around the bowl of water.
Be sure to have at least one for each person.

OPENING SONG: Glory to God

This is a song for two groups to sing in two parts that almost, but not quite, echo one another.
Sing it through at least three times.

Glory to God;
Praise to the Son;
Love to the Spirit;
Three and yet One.

> — John L. Bell, Iona Community, *Wonder, Love, and Praise*, #821

JOHN 4:1–30, 39–42   The Samaritan Woman at the Well

This story works well as a dramatic reading, with different readers for the narrator, the Samaritan woman,
Jesus, the disciples, the Samaritans.

Now when Jesus learned that the Pharisees had heard,
      "Jesus is making and baptizing more disciples than John"
—although it was not Jesus himself but his disciples who baptized—
      he left Judea and started back to Galilee. But he had to go through Samaria.
So he came to a Samaritan city called Sychar,
      near the plot of ground that Jacob had given to his son Joseph.
Jacob's well was there, and Jesus, tired out by his journey,
      was sitting by the well. It was about noon.
A Samaritan woman came to draw water, and Jesus said to her,
      "Give me a drink." (His disciples had gone to the city to buy food.)

The Samaritan woman said to him,
      "How is it that you, a Jew, ask a drink of me, a woman of Samaria?"
(Jews do not share things in common with Samaritans.)

Jesus answered her,

    "If you knew the gift of God, and who it is that is saying to you, 'Give me a drink,'
    you would have asked him and he would have given you living water."

The woman said to him,

    "Sir, you have no bucket, and the well is deep.
    Where do you get that living water?
    Are you greater than our ancestor Jacob, who gave us the well,
    and with his sons and his flocks drank from it?"

Jesus said to her,

    "Everyone who drinks of this water will be thirsty again,
      but those who drink of the water that I will give them will never be thirsty.
    The water that I will give will become in them a spring of water gushing up to eternal life."

The woman said to him,

    "Sir, give me this water, so that I may never be thirsty
      or have to keep coming here to draw water."

Jesus said to her,

    "Go, call your husband, and come back."

The woman answered him,

    "I have no husband."

Jesus said to her,

    "You are right in saying, 'I have no husband';
      for you have had five husbands,
      and the one you have now is not your husband.
    What you have said is true!"

The woman said to him,

    "Sir, I see that you are a prophet.
    Our ancestors worshiped on this mountain,
      but you say that the place where people must worship is in Jerusalem."

Jesus said to her,

    "Woman, believe me,
      the hour is coming when you will worship the Father
      neither on this mountain nor in Jerusalem.
    You worship what you do not know; we worship what we know,
      for salvation is from the Jews.

But the hour is coming, and is now here,
    when the true worshipers will worship the Father in spirit and truth,
    for the Father seeks such as these to worship him. God is spirit,
    and those who worship him must worship him in spirit and truth."

The woman said to him,
    "I know that the Messiah is coming" (who is called Christ).
    "When he comes, he will proclaim all things to us."
Jesus said to her,
    "I am he, the one who is speaking to you."

Just then his disciples came.
They were astonished that he was speaking with a woman,
      but no one said, "What do you want?" or,
    "Why are you speaking with her?"

Then the woman left her water jar and went back to the city.
She said to the people,
    "Come and see a man who told me everything
      I have ever done!
    He cannot be the Messiah, can he?"

They left the city and were on their way to him.

Many Samaritans from that city believed in him because of the
    woman's testimony,
    "He told me everything I have ever done."
So when the Samaritans came to him, they asked him
      to stay with them;
    and he stayed there two days.
And many believed because of his word.
They said to the woman,
    "It is no longer because of what you said that we believe,
      for we have heard for ourselves,
      and we know that this is truly the Savior of the world."

Psalm 63:1–8

*At the end of each sentence or phrase followed by a line space,
have the group speak together "O God, you are my God."*

O God, you are my God; eagerly I seek you;
  my soul thirsts for you, my flesh faints for you,
  as in a barren and dry land where there is no water.

Therefore I have gazed upon you in your holy place,
  that I might behold your power and your glory.

For your loving-kindness is better than life itself;
  my lips shall give you praise.

So will I bless you as long as I live
  and lift up my hands in your Name.

My soul is content, as with marrow and fatness,
  and my mouth praises you with joyful lips,

When I remember you upon my bed,
  and meditate on you in the night watches.

For you have been my helper,
  and under the shadow of your wings I will rejoice.

My soul clings to you;
  your right hand holds me fast.

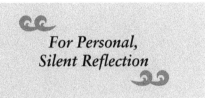

For Personal, Silent Reflection

It is noon, the hottest time of the day. The Samaritan woman goes to the well for water and is surprised by Jesus. Spend a few moments in silence wondering about the following:

Why did she come to the well at this time of the day?

What were her feelings as Jesus first spoke with her?

What were her thirsts?

What were her feelings and thirsts at the end of the encounter?

How was she changed?
  How was Jesus changed?

What impact might the experience have had on the rest of her life?

Imagine yourself in the place of the Samaritan woman:

What is your greatest thirst?
  How might you quench it?

By looking at your life, what would people think is your thirst?

What gets in the way of your drinking of the living water?

Have you recently encountered someone who is outcast in your society?

How could you show Jesus to them?

What living water do you have to share?

Lord's Prayer

This version can be sung using Wonder, Love, and Praise *settings #833 or #864.*

Our Father in heaven,
    hallowed be your Name,
    your kingdom come,
    your will be done,
        on earth as in heaven.
Give us today our daily bread.
Forgive us our sins
    as we forgive those
        who sin against us.
Save us from the time of trial
    and deliver us from evil.
For the kingdom, the power,
    and the glory are yours,
        now and for ever. Amen.

Collect

Almighty and everlasting God,
you have given to us your servants grace,
by the confession of a true faith,
to acknowledge the glory of the eternal Trinity,
and in the power of your divine Majesty to worship
    the Unity:
Keep us steadfast in this faith and worship,
and bring us at last to see you in your one and
    eternal glory,
O Father; who with the Son and the Holy Spirit
    live and reign,
one God, for ever and ever. Amen.

— First Sunday after Pentecost: Trinity Sunday,
The Book of Common Prayer, p. 228

The word for "believe" is a compound symbol composed of a radical (root) for "human" (see the legs of a person standing) next to the word for speech (there is an open mouth at the bottom). This word might also be translated as "trust" in English. Unlike the English definition of "believe," this word implies activity.

Sharing

DAD WAS DYING. It was the end of his thirty-six-year journey with Parkinson's disease. With Hospice help, he was home with us, and we were thankful. My sister had come up from Raleigh with her two children—Will, an infant, and Mary, four years old. We wondered how to explain to Mary what was happening to her grandfather. We decided simply to answer the questions she asked, and so, when she eventually asked what was wrong with Grampy, our response was,

"Grampy's body, his shell, is old and sick. It will die soon. But when that happens, his real self can go be with God."

It was a beautiful June day when Dad died. We were out in the yard watching them take his "shell" away. A stiff wind came by, blowing a flurry of white petals off a nearby fruit tree. As the petals whirled all around us, Mary looked up with a smile on her face, raised her arms high and proclaimed with utmost surety, "Mommy! Look! It's the angels taking Grampy's real self home to God!"

Esperanza Means Hope

— by Kathleen M. Bozzuti-Jones

ONE DAY, I WAS a newlywed delighted to have discovered that we were expecting a baby. The next day, I was a medical case study with the rarest of conditions. I was informed that, in order to regain full health, I would have to carry the tiny baby within me for six months after he had died. This sentence of discomfort and aching sadness was more than I was prepared to handle gracefully. And so I had fallen into a hole of self-pity and brooding that I could not seem to rise above, despite my husband's attention and consolation. In my misery, I could not pray, and, if God was speaking to me, I did not want to hear it.

Shortly after the six months had passed, I received a surprise invitation to travel to Honduras on a mission trip with the Episcopal Diocese of Massachusetts' Youth Leadership Academy. The group carried with them two years of preparation for their trip, along with bundles of collected donations. With two days' notice, I brought only my heartache and a keen desire to turn my gaze outward in service.

So it was that on one hot June afternoon in the capital city of Tegucigalpa, we set out to visit local parishioners. Along the way, we stopped at the tiny shack of Esperanza, an elderly woman who lived by the road, down a steep dirt path, with three generations of family members. She welcomed us to sit on the dusty ground as she tended to some food on the wood stove. Esperanza began to tell us of her recent illness, describing in detail the pain and delirium she had experienced. And she told us of her miracle: how she had died and then returned. She told us that she is alive today because God heard the prayers of her church community.

Esperanza's daughter stood near the door, listening, nodding, and tending to her small children. Her childlike face was serene and sober. Esperanza told us that this daughter had been raped on the road, while carrying some wood—and a daughter of her own *in utero*. At this point, I was sickened as I began to grasp the vulnerability and lack of recourse that permeated their poverty.

I collected myself enough to utter a string of petitions, asking God for relief from their fear, their hunger, and their pain. When I had finished, Esperanza indicated that she wanted to continue the prayer. She raised her hands to her face, covered her eyes, and began to wail, an outpouring that seemed to come from the bottom of a deep well. I will never forget the sound of it, nor will I forget the first words that followed—words of thanksgiving. Thanksgiving! While I was fixated on her suffering, Esperanza's heart was fixed on thanking her generous and loving Father. The sound of her cry, the tenacity of her faith, and the indictment of my own failure to give thanks for my health and my privilege welled up in my heart throughout that day.

I had come to this house hoping to offer some company and support. Instead, I left feeling as though I had drunk deeply from the well of Esperanza's intimate knowledge of God's goodness. In that tiny shack filled with gratitude, faith, fellowship, and solidarity, I found healing. In the well of Esperanza's gratitude, I found my hope in God's goodness again.

For Small Group Discussion

Go to the bowl of water and look at the crosses that are arranged around it. Find one that speaks to you. Pick it up and spend some moments in contemplation of it. After everyone has chosen a cross and is seated, share your responses to the following with another person:

Why did you choose that particular cross?

Do you wear a cross? If so, show it, and tell why you wear it.

Where did you get the cross?

Think about the contents of your home.

Are there any sacred objects there that speak of your faith? Choose one and describe it.

Where is it placed?

Where did you get it?

What does it represent?

When and why do you display it?

Share a time when your faith was challenged.

Did it change or affirm anything about what you believe?

Who or what helped in your exploration?

And It Was Heaven

AS A CHILD we made regular trips from my small farming community in Ohio, to Columbus. We would go for doctor appointments or concerts, but most often it was to shop. So much so that my dad used to joke that the low gear "L" on the transmission stick was for Lazarus, the big six floor department store. They even had an annex, and their own parking garage! And Santa was there at Christmas time, and there was a Christmas store that only children could go into to buy gifts!

On one of the trips, as we turned a corner, I looked up at a building ahead at the end of the street, pointed to a large statue above its door. It was large, pot-bellied man who had a crown on his head. One arm was raised in the air, the other held a scepter. I am told that upon seeing it, I pointed and proclaimed, with eyes wide open "Mommy, Look! There's God!!"

I now know that the building was a brewery. The large white man over the door was their logo, a fat, drunk king. The raised arm was holding a mug of beer! So much for an image of God.

Who is God to me now? Recently, I awoke one day with a song in my head, and it was a worm that appeared every morning for weeks after that. It was a Bette Midler song with the refrain "God

is watching us. God is watching us, God is watching us, from a distance." I realized I don't like that song at all. If feels obtrusive, like God is stalking us. And for me, God is not at a distance! So why was it hounding me?

There is a woman I have known for years. Her name is Heather. She is a diminutive, red-haired spirit who lives with a severe mental illness. She is often on the street, wearing layers of clothes, carrying bags of belongings with her. From time to time, she devolves enough that the local mental health crisis unit can get her into the hospital. Once stabilized, she is able to be placed in an apartment and for a while, maintains that safety. That is until a boyfriend re-appears and drags her back into her psychosis. Life falls apart and she appears again on the street.

Heather started coming to the women's center years ago to take a shower and for a change of clothes. During the height of the pandemic, that was no longer an option, but recently I saw her sitting in the middle of the sidewalk near where I live. All her belongings were scattered around her and she was shouting at someone who was not there—or at least someone I could not see. It was about the time that Bette Midler's song would not leave my subconscious mind.

I was walking to my church on an errand and passed her by on the other side of the street. On my way home, Heather was still there. This time I paused, walked over to her, leaned down to her level and spoke her name. There was no answer. Again, "Heather, it's Klara." Nothing. Again "Heather, it's me, Klara from the women's center. I haven't seen you in awhile. Do you remember me?"

After the third try, she looked up, her eyes cleared and she smiled and in a softer voice "Oh, yes!" I asked how she was doing. "Not so good, I got a lot of problems" and she proceeded to list them. She asked me when the food pantry would be open, and I told her. She had a bowl of water between her legs and a rag in her hand. She told me she was waiting for the pantry and meanwhile was just washing up. With the women's center now open again, I reminded her about the shower. "No, I don't take showers anymore, I just carry my bath water with me." she said as she began to wash her face.

The moment of connection faded as she got back to her business. "You take care Heather" I said "I will pray for you." And I did pray for her, off and on throughout the rest of the afternoon, whenever I heard her shouting and howling.

Who is God in the midst of that? Where is God? I have to believe that Jesus, the incarnate God was present, sitting there with Heather, and maybe even talking with her. And me? The Spirit, Wisdom, Sophia compelled me to pay attention and go join them. Even if just for a brief moment, there we were, all together, sitting on the sidewalk, and it was heaven.

Reflecting

Scripture

Exodus 3:13–15   God's name revealed

Daniel 6:10–28   Daniel in the lions' den

Psalm 42:1–7   As the deer longs for the water-brooks

Matthew 14:22–33   Jesus and Peter walk on water

Matthew 15:21–28   Canaanite Woman
(also Mark 7:24–30)

Matthew 16:13–23   Who do you say that I am?
(also Mark 8:27–30; Luke 9:18–20)

Matthew 17:20   Faith small as mustard seed
(also Luke 17:6)

Matthew 26:69–75   Peter's denial
(also Mark 14:66–72; Luke 22:54–62;
*   John 18:15–18, 25–27)*

Mark 5:25–34   Hemorrhaging woman healed
(also Matthew 9:20–22; Luke 8:43–48)

Mark 9:14–29   I believe; help my unbelief

Mark 10:13–16   Jesus blesses little children
(also Matthew 19:13–15; Luke 18:15–17)

Mark 10:46–52   Healing of blind Bartimaeus
(also Matthew 20:29–34; Luke 18:35–43)

Mark 11:20–14   Withered fig tree
(also Matthew 21:20–22)

Luke 1:46–55   The Magnificat
(also Luke 2:68–79; 3:29–32)

John 1:1–5   The word became flesh
(see Genesis 1:1–5)

John 9:35–41   Spiritual blindness

John 12:44–50   The unbelief of people

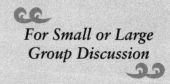

For Small or Large Group Discussion

Refer to the scripture selections. Choose one or two that speak to you, and discuss them.

What word or phrase jumps out at you?

What does the passage say to you?

What is it calling you to do?

Consider any of the suggested hymns that relate to your conversation.
Read over the Prayer Book selections and comments.

What light do they shed on your conversation?

John 14:1–14   I am the way
John 20:24–29   Thomas' doubt
Hebrews 11   Meaning of faith

Hymns

The Hymnal 1982
   "The Holy Trinity" section, #362–371
   Creating God, your fingers trace, #394, #395
   The first one ever, #673
   Oh sons and daughters let us sing, #206
   We Walk by Faith, #209

Wonder, Love, and Praise
   I am the bread of life, #762
   If you believe and I believe, #806
   I believe in God almighty, #768, #769
   God the sculptor of the mountains, #746, #747
   Sh'ma Yisrael, #818

The New Century Hymnal
   Bring many names, #11
   Praise with joy the world's Creator, #273
   Womb of life, and source of being, #274
   Creator God, creating still, #278

The Book of Common Prayer

The Catechism:
   God the Father, p. 846
   God the Son, pp. 849–850
   The Creeds, pp. 851–852
   The Holy Spirit, pp. 852–853
The Creeds:
   The Apostles' Creed, p. 53 (traditional),
      p. 96 (contemporary)
   The Nicene Creed, pp. 326–327
   The Creed of Saint Athanasius, pp. 864–865

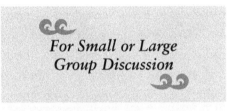

For Small or Large Group Discussion

Describe a time when you were surprised
   by an encounter with God.
   Or, describe a relationship with someone
   that gave you a glimpse of the Holy and
   nurtured your faith.

   How did the encounter challenge you?

   How were you changed?

   Did your image of God change?

   How is your image of God different now
      than when you were a child?

Remember a time when you denied or
   doubted God. Describe it.

   How did you work through the doubt?

   In the historic creeds, what is the hardest
      thing for you to believe?

The first three question-and-answer segments of the Baptismal Covenant are based on the Apostles' Creed. They form a statement of belief by describing and defining images for God's nature—Father, Son, and Holy Spirit. Some of the earliest professions of faith are found in the first chapter of John and in the Epistles (Romans 10:9–10; 1 Corinthians 8:6; Ephesians 4:5; 1 Peter 1:3–5; Colossians 1:15–20; and Philippians 2:6–11).

The creeds as we know them today resulted from the Councils of Nicea (325 c.e.), Constantinople (381 c.e.), Ephesus (431 c.e.), and Calcedon (451 c.e.). They express the understandings of the winners of the theological battles of their day.

When we think of the Baptismal Covenant, we tend to gloss over the three creedal questions and jump to the five questions that follow—which define how to live what we profess. A friend of mine, Holly, says that skipping over the creed is a mistake. She explains that creeds give shape to our belief in God. They are the traditional, historic stones around the well that make us able to access the living water. You could also say the creeds are the banks of the river or shore of the sea. They provide a container we need as human beings. From that container we can drink, and come to discover and better understand our faith. We can respond in our life accordingly. As a result, the creeds have consistently been used as the core of baptismal instruction.

On the other hand, faith doesn't derive from past history, theology, or dogma alone. Somewhere, I have heard the phrase "Jesus seldom said believe in me, but he did often say follow me." Jesus was the word made flesh, who dwelt among us. God not only exists, but God loves us and is with us. The creeds talk about the God in whom we believe. Faith is more about talking with the God to whom we give our heart. I can believe someone exists, but not have faith in him or her. I can know about—but not really know—someone. Faith arises out of relationship with God and with other believers. It is as much a matter of the heart as of the head. The relationship, based in trust and love, brings an indescribable knowing that grows and changes over time. The frequently used Hebrew word for this "knowing" of someone was "Yada." The word implies a deep and evolving relationship, based in a sensuous love.

So, while the creeds as we know them are a valuable container, we also should note that the last creed was written 1,500 years ago. It is as if our understanding of God was frozen in time. Some say we need to develop new images for God. Monica Hellwig, for example, posits that Jesus could be considered the incarnate "Compassion of God." While holding to the historic creeds, can we create new versions? Would new images suited to our time in history better enable us to put on the mind of Christ and help us live as faithful disciples?

Reflectively read one or two of the following quotes. What is your response?

The central issue of the Christian life is not about believing in God or believing in the Bible or believing in Christian tradition. Rather, the Christian life is about entering into a relationship with that to which the Christian tradition points, which may be spoken of as God, the risen living Christ or the Spirit.... My own journey has led beyond belief ... to a relationship that involves one in a journey of transformation.

— Marcus J. Borg, *Meeting Jesus Again for the First Time*, p. 17

If you took the Trinity as a work of the imagination, rather than clobbering people with a dogma that they can't even begin to talk about, you would come up with a very different kind of conversation.... [Christianity] is not an argument. And God is not an idea, not even a good one. God is not a concept. In other words, my first thing is wanting to talk to people not about God, but about their passions and their enthusiasms, about their fears, their moral imagination and their emotional life. I don't mean emotionalism, but I mean their life of affect in the world. And then we can give the word "God" some content!

— Alan Jones, in *The Witness*, vol. 84, no. 718, August 2001, p. 14

After many years of vain attempts to "explain" God as trinity, I now say, "Well, to begin with we Christians have been taught to pray, 'Our Father, who art in heaven ...'" I then suggest that a good place to begin to understand what we Christians are about is to join me in that prayer.

— Stanley Hauerwas, *After Christendom?*; as quoted in
A Sourcebook about Liturgy, Liturgy Training Publications, p. 105

When, Like the Woman at the Well

When, like the woman at the well,
I lived with broken dreams,
Christ came to me, good news to tell,
of ever-living streams.

Christ knew my heart, my wayward ways,
yet gave me hope, not fear.
The God I once thought far away,
I could approach, draw near.

I learned I could forever live
and worship God aright,
could trust the power the Spirit gives
to guide me in truth's light.

Each day I lift my cup above,
and I again receive
the living water of God's love,
revealed for my belief.

Since now I am in grace immersed,
set free, forgiven, whole,
I share with those who are athirst
the well-springs of my soul!

> — Edith Sinclair Downing,
> *The New Century Hymnal*, #196

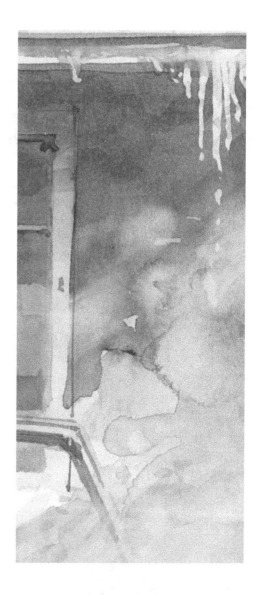

... but Moses said to God, "If I come to the Israelites and say to them, 'The God of your ancestors has sent me to you,' and they ask me, 'What is his name?' what shall I say to them?" God said to Moses, "I AM WHO I AM." He said further, "Thus you shall say to the Israelites, 'I AM has sent me to you.'" God also said to Moses, "Thus you shall say to the Israelites, 'The LORD, the God of your ancestors, the God of Abraham, the God of Isaac, and the God of Jacob, has sent me to you': This is my name forever, and this my title for all generations."

> — Exodus 3:13–15

As children of God, we affirm:

That God, who is Love, created all and called it good, that God is present with all of creation, and that, in darkness and in light, God is faithful; therefore we, too, seek to be faithful.

That Jesus came to show us Love with a human face, that he taught justice and reconciliation and suffered on our behalf, and that through his faithful example, he embodies hope; therefore we, too, seek to be people of justice, reconciliation, and hope.

That the Holy Spirit guides and accompanies us, that this same Spirit offers wisdom and discernment, and that, when we are open, the Spirit can always find a way; therefore, we seek to be people filled with God's Spirit: discerning, loving and transforming our world. Amen.

— *Daily Prayer for All Seasons*, Church Publishing

I am the bread of life. Whoever comes to me will never be hungry, and whoever believes in me will never be thirsty.

— John 6:35

I am the light of the world. Whoever follows me will never walk in darkness but will have the light of life.

— John 8:12

I am the way, and the truth, and the life. No one comes to the Father except through me.

— John 14:6

I am the true vine, and my Father is the vinegrower....
I am the vine, you are the branches.

— John 15:1, 5

I am the resurrection and the life. Those who believe in me, even though they die, will live, and everyone who lives and believes in me will never die.

— John 11:25–26

Meditations on the Names of God

To you who laid the foundations of the earth, I dare speak.

We have called you by many names,
in many languages, through many centuries.

Here in this transition time, none of those names seems sufficient,
expressive, easy to speak when I try to bring myself before you.

"Jesus," I can say, no problem—wind and fire anointing the Apostles,
your still voice at the center of the whirlwind,
caretaker of this strange thing we call the Church.

But what of you, O first person of the Trinity?

If I don't pay attention during church
I can roll through all those names without a hitch:
Father, Lord, King.

But when I hear myself, or focus on the words upon the page,
I falter, resisting the baggage of human fathers, lords, kings.

But human baggage cannot weigh you down.

You were enigmatic when directly asked your name:
just "I AM, tell them I AM sent you."
what kind of name is that? I AM what?

Is this an elaborate game
in which the goal is to discover what is hidden?
Or do we know instinctively
that to name something is to control it
as Adam named the animals?

Is that why your name is a mystery,
must remain a mystery,
lest we imagine even for a moment
we can control your beauty and your power?

God forbid,

Speak my name, lover of souls, that I may be wholly yours.
Then none of the rest will matter at all.

— Pamela W. Darling, *Women's Uncommon Prayer*, p. 213

Karl Barth, when asked if he could summarize what he had said in all his theological writings, replied: "Jesus loves me! This I know, for the Bible tells me so."

Jesus Loves Me

Jesus loves me! This I know,
    for the Bible tells me so.
Little ones to him belong;
    they are weak, but he is strong.

Jesus loves me! This I know,
    as he loved so long ago,
Taking children on his knee,
    saying, "Let them come to me."

Jesus loves me! Still today,
    walking with me on my way,
Wanting as a friend to give
    light and love to all who live.

Refrain:
Yes, Jesus loves me!
Yes, Jesus loves me!
Yes, Jesus loves me!
The Bible tells me so.
    — Anna B. Warner (stanza 1),
      David Rutherford McGuire (stanzas 2–3),
      The New Century Hymnal, #327

"Jesus Loves Me"
— Armenian transliteration Vartan Hartunian
Deer He-soos zis guh see-reh,
    eem soorp keer-kus ice guh-seh,
Inch koo-tov ink un-toon-etz
    po-ker dug-hak, yev orh-netz.

    Vo, guh see-reh ziss!
    Vo, guh see-reh ziss!
    Vo, guh see-reh ziss!
    Soorp Kirk-uh ice guh-seh.

"Jesus Loves Me"
— Spanish translation, *Himnario Metodista*, 1968
Cris-to me a-ma, bien lo sé,
    Su pa-la-bra me ha-ce ver
Que los ni-ños son de A-quél,
    Quien es nues-tro A-mi-go fiel.

    Cris-to me a-ma,
    Cris-to me a-ma,
    Cris-to me a-ma,
    La Bib-lia di-ce a-sí

"Jesus Loves Me"
—Lakota translation, Dakota Odowan, 1842
Je-sus Christ wa- śte-ma-da,
    Wo-wa-pi Wa-kan he-ye:
Mi-ye on te hi qon he,
    Wan-na he wa-na-ka-ja.

    Han Je-sus wa-śte;
    Han Je-sus wa-śte;
    Han Je-sus wa-śte;
    Wa-śte ma-da-ka ye.

"Jesus Loves Me"
— Samoan translation, anonymous
Lo'u A-lii ua faa-fe-tai
    I lou sa-ga a-lo-fa-mai,
Ua i-lo-a-ti-no ai
    I lou tau-si pe-a mai.

    O lou a-lo-fa!
    O lou a-lo-fa!
    O lou a-lo-fa!
    E si-li la-va lea.

"Jesus Loves Me"
— Japanese phonetic transcription, Mas Kawashima, 1988
Saq wa-re o a-i-su,
    Saq wa tsu-yo ke-re ba,
Wa-re yo-wa-ku-to-mo,
    O-so-re wa a-ra-ji.

    Wa-ga Shu ye-su,
    Wa-ga Shu ye-su,
    Wa-ga Shu ye-su,
    Wa-re o a-i-su.

"Jesus Loves Me"
—Hungarian translation, János Victor
En-gem sze-ret Jé-zu-som,
    Bib-li-ám-ból jól tu-dom.
Mind ö-vé a kis gyer-mek,
    E-rőt ád a gyön gék-nek!

    Úgy van ő sze-ret,
    Ő sze-ret na-gyon;
    Úgy van ő sze-ret,
    Í-gé-jé-ből tudom.

— translations from *The New Century Hymnal*, #327

I Heard the Voice of Jesus Say

I heard the voice of Jesus say,
    "Come unto me and rest;
lay down, O weary one, lay down
    your head upon my breast."

I came to Jesus as I was,
    so weary, worn, and sad,
and there I found a resting place,
    where Jesus made me glad!

I heard the voice of Jesus say,
    "Behold, I freely give
the living water; thirsty one,
    draw near, and drink, and live."

I came to Jesus, and I drank
    of that life-giving stream;
my thirst was quenched, my soul revived,
    and now I am redeemed.

I heard the voice of Jesus say,
    "I am this lost world's Light,
Look unto me; your morn shall rise,
    and all your day be bright."

I looked to Jesus, and I found
    my guiding Star, my Sun;
and in that light of life I'll go
    till traveling days are done.

                   — Horatius Bonar

I believe in the sun

    Even when it is not shining.

I believe in love

    Even when feeling it not.

I believe in God

    Even when God is silent.

                — a wall inscription found by Allied
                  troops in 1945; attributed to an
                  anonymous Holocaust victim

Responding

Practicing Together:

• Divide all the Psalms evenly among the participants. You can use either biblical texts or The Psalter in the Book of Common Prayer (pp. 585–808). Scan the assigned Psalms and quickly record the images for God that they find. Compile all the images on newsprint. Discuss your favorites. Which ones surprised you? What are some images you would add to the list?

— An activity learned in a workshop led by Donald Griggs

• If Jesus asked you the question, "Who do you say that I am?" how would you respond? Or, if a nonbeliever asked you to explain what you believe and why, what would you say? Take a moment to write notes about what your response might be. Share your answers with another person in the group.

• Look at a wide range of styles of paintings and sculptures that depict God, Jesus, or the Holy Spirit. Which visual images do you like? Which offend you? Why? What is your favorite painting or sculpture that depicts God? Create an image out of air-dry clay that expresses your faith or your image of God at the moment. Share your images with each other, then take them home.

• Read Hebrews 11:1–3. Ask everyone to write down a completion of the sentence "Faith is …" Then compile the sentences on newsprint. Discuss the meaning of faith.

Practicing at Home:

• Read the creed on p. 51 as a sample of an alternative to the Apostles, and Nicean creeds. In your journal, write a creed for yourself that is a personal vision reflecting our contemporary world. Recite it daily. How is it the same as the Nicene or Apostles' Creed? How is it different? Take your creed back to the group and compare them. You can do so anonymously by posting them, unsigned, on the wall. Discuss differences and similarities.

• Place objects on your home altar that express what you believe. Hang images on your doors and on your walls that mark your house as a faith-filled place.

• If you have not done so, consider having a house blessing. Write your own liturgy, or adapt the "Celebration for a Home" liturgy found in the Pastoral Services section of *The Book of Occasional Services.*

- Every morning, read the Psalm appointed for the day. Whenever "he" is used in reference to God, simply speak the word "God" instead. Do this for a number of weeks. Read some translations of the Psalms that substitute the Hebrew word Yahweh or other words for "God." Take note of your feelings about doing this. What name do you most often use for God?

- Meditate on the passage John 14:1–7. Take note of the context, the question Thomas asks. Read verse 6 three times, with a different emphasis each time: "*I* am the way ... I *am* the way ... I am *the way*." What difference does each reading make in the meaning of the phrase? What do you think Jesus intended? Why?

- Put a small cross in your pocket or change purse, or on a key chain. Say a short prayer of adoration every time you touch it.

Closing Prayers

Sing again the Opening Song, "Glory to God," which was sung in the time of Gathering.
Take a moment to share thanksgivings and personal prayer needs.
Close with the following prayer and blessing.

Everlasting God, who strengthened your apostle Thomas with firm and certain faith in your Son's resurrection: Grant us so perfectly and without doubt to believe in Jesus Christ, our Lord and our God, that our faith may never be found wanting in your sight; through him who lives and reigns with you and the Holy Spirit, one God, now and for ever. Amen.

— collect for the feast of Saint Thomas, The Book of Common Prayer, p. 237

The Lord God Almighty, Father, Son, and Holy Spirit, the holy and undivided Trinity, guard us, save us, and bring us to that heavenly City, where he lives and reigns for ever and ever. Amen.

— "Seasonal Blessings," The First Sunday after Pentecost:
Trinity Sunday, *The Book of Occasional Services,* p. 26 (adapted)

July 21

Went back near the nest this morning, this time with binoculars
and Mom's camera with a telephoto lens. The nest has been
abandoned with an egg still in it. I felt sad to think that the loons
gave up—that there would be no chicks this year. But then, just
around the next cove, there was the pair with a chick! There must
have been two eggs, and only one hatched. The little one is so tiny!
I have never seen one this small. It jumps on and off the mother's
back and bobs around beside her.

Session Three

Will you continue in the apostles' teaching and fellowship, in the breaking of bread, and in the prayers?

Gathering

Place a large, round loaf of bread in a basket in the center of the circle, next to the bowl of water.
If possible lay a sheaf of wheat next to the bread. You might include a bunch of grapes in the basket with the bread.

OPENING SONG: **The Disciples Knew the Lord Jesus**

For this song, use one of the musical settings found in Wonder, Love, and Praise, *#875–877.*
Teach the antiphon to the group. They sing it at the beginning, between the two verses, and again at the end.
A solo cantor sings the verses.

Antiphon: The disciples knew the Lord Jesus in the breaking of the bread.

The bread which we break, Alleluia,
    Is the communion of the Body of Christ.

One body are we, Alleluia,
    For though many we share one bread.

JOHN 21:1–18   **Jesus Appears to the Disciples**

Arrange for the parts of the disciples, Jesus, and Peter to be spoken as a dramatic dialogue.
Have a recording of water sounds playing in the background.

Jesus showed himself again to the disciples by the Sea of Tiberias; and he showed himself in this way. Gathered there together were Simon Peter, Thomas called the Twin, Nathanael of Cana in Galilee, the sons of Zebedee, and two others of his disciples.

Simon Peter said to them, "I am going fishing."
They said to him. "We will go with you."

They went out and got into the boat, but that night they caught nothing. Just after daybreak, Jesus stood on the beach; but the disciples did not know that it was Jesus.

Jesus said to them, "Children, you have no fish, have you?"

They answered him, "No."

He said to them, "Cast your net to the right side of the boat, and you will find some."

So they cast it, and now they were not able to haul it in because there were so many fish.

That disciple whom Jesus loved said to Peter, "It is the Lord!"

When Simon Peter heard that it was the Lord, he put on some clothes, for he was naked, and jumped into the sea. But the other disciples came in the boat, dragging the net full of fish, for they were not far from the land, only about a hundred yards off. When they had gone ashore, they saw a charcoal fire there, with fish on it, and bread.

Jesus said to them, "Bring some of the fish that you have just caught."

So Simon Peter went aboard and hauled the net ashore, full of large fish, a hundred fifty-three of them; and though there were so many, the net was not torn.

Jesus said to them, "Come and have breakfast."

Now none of the disciples dared to ask him, "Who are you?" because they knew it was the Lord. Jesus came and took the bread and gave it to them, and did the same with the fish. This was now the third time that Jesus appeared to the disciples after he was raised from the dead.

When they had finished breakfast, Jesus said to Simon Peter,
    "Simon son of John, do you love me more than these?"
He said to him, "Yes, Lord; you know that I love you."
Jesus said to him, "Feed my lambs."

A second time he said to him, "Simon, son of John, do you love me?"
He said to him, "Yes, Lord; you know that I love you."
Jesus said to him, "Tend my sheep."

He said to him the third time, "Simon, son of John, do you love me?"
Peter felt hurt because he said to him the third time,
    "Do you love me?" And he said to him,
    "Lord, you know everything; you know that I love you."
Jesus said to him, "Feed my sheep."

Soon after Jesus' crucifixion, the disciples go out fishing all night, but they catch nothing. In the morning, Jesus, whom they do not recognize, calls to them from the beach, telling them to cast their net on the right (to them, the wrong) side of the boat. When they do, not only do they catch more fish than they can haul in, but they also realize who is speaking to them. Jesus calls them ashore. When they reach him, he is cooking fish and bread over a charcoal fire.

Imagine standing there on the beach
with Jesus and the disciples.
Spend a few moments in silence
wondering about the following:

What are the disciples feeling?

What previous encounter with Jesus are they remembering?

Jesus turns and thrice asks Peter if he loves him.

What memory does the conversation evoke in Peter?

What are you thinking and feeling as you stand there?

If Jesus asked you "Do you love me?" how would you respond?
How might you show it?

Psalm 23

Read this psalm together, or you can sing hymn #645 or #664 in The Hymnal 1982.

The LORD is my shepherd;
    I shall not be in want.

He makes me lie down in green pastures
    and leads me beside still waters.

He revives my soul
    and guides me along right pathways for
    his Name's sake.

Though I walk through the valley of the shadow
    of death,
I shall fear no evil;
    for you are with me;
    your rod and your staff, they comfort me.

You spread a table before me in the presence
    of those who trouble me;
    you have anointed my head with oil,
    and my cup is running over.

Surely your goodness and mercy shall follow me
    all the days of my life,
    and I will dwell in the house of the LORD for ever.

The Lord's Prayer

Eternal Spirit,
Earth-maker, Pain-bearer, Life-giver,
Source of all that is and that shall be,
Father and Mother of us all,
Loving God, in whom is heaven:

The hallowing of your name echo through the universe!
The way of your justice be followed by the peoples of the world!
Your heavenly will be done by all created beings!
Your commonwealth of peace and freedom sustain our hope
    and come on earth.

With the bread we need for today, feed us.
In the hurts we absorb from one another, forgive us.
In times of temptation and test, strengthen us.
From trials too great to endure, spare us.
From the grip of all that is evil, free us.

For you reign in the glory of the power that is love,
    Now and for ever. Amen.

            — A New Zealand Prayer Book, p. 181

Collect

O God, whose blessed Son
    made himself known to his disciples
    in the breaking of the bread:
Open the eyes of our faith,
    that we may behold him in all his redeeming work;
    who lives and reigns with you, in the unity of the Holy Spirit,
    one God, now and forever. Amen.

      — Third Sunday of Easter, The Book of Common Prayer, p. 224

Sharing

THIS MORNING was my weekly trip to the Black Crow Bakery. It is a small, family-run business in Litchfield, Maine. They bake breads much as their Greek grandfather did, with freshly milled flour, slow rising, natural starters, in a wood burning brick oven. Among the dozen breads they bake, my family's favorites are the olive herb, apricot almond, pane siciliano, and brown rice sesame breads. The sticky-sweet cranberry walnut rolls are to die for! You have to go early in the day. By noon most of the bread is gone.

The bakery is in an antique farmhouse, on a side road, near the fairgrounds, just past the Blue Whale Berry Farm. There is usually a chicken roosting in a flowerpot by the door, an old dog sleeping in the yard. The door to the bakery is between the house and garage. On the way in you pass the back of the old brick oven, a pile of logs beside it. Inside a radio is quietly playing music, and beside the oven is a shelf of breads with a utility light trained on it. Flour dusts the floor and sticks to the soles of your shoes. If you arrive by eight in the morning, the breads and the oven are still warm, and the aroma heavenly. The loaves are all labeled with a descriptive name and a price. You choose what you want, and leave money in a cookie tin. No one, of course, takes advantage of the situation. I did once see a woman take some bread without paying, but she explained to me that she barters eggs from her farm for bread.

There is no one around. The loaves of bread—like the shoes in the Hans Christian Andersen story about the shoemaker and the elves—just magically appear in the night. It never fails. To this day, no one in my family has ever seen the baker, but the bread is always there.

MY COMMUNITY of faith as a child was the Mound Street Presbyterian Church in Circleville, Ohio. Church involvement was an ever-present part of our family's life. Carol and Wally Higgins were often my Sunday school teachers. Their quiet and consistent presence deeply formed me in faith. This was especially true of Carol who was also the junior choir director. To this day, when I hear the anthem "The Prayer of St. Richard of Chichester," I think of her. "Day by day, dear Lord, of thee three things I pray: to see thee more clearly, love thee more dearly, follow thee more nearly, day by day." When I was a bit older, Carol taught me to play the recorder, first my little soprano flute, then her large tenor one. She let me practice with her ensemble of adult members, and even let me perform with them.

I remember one particular Sunday encounter with Carol. It had nothing to do with Sunday school or choir. I was about ten years old, and it was around the time of my dad's first brain surgery. It was after worship, and as we were leaving the sanctuary. Carol and I became so engrossed in conversation that we settled ourselves on the top step of the three stairs that led out of the church. The whole congregation was rushing past us, but we sat in deep conversation, oblivious to them. *What* we were saying wasn't as important to this story as *how* we were saying it: an adult and a ten-year-old were eye to eye, suspended in time, completely caught up in one another's lives.

I FINALLY MET THE RABBI who lives two doors down. When moving into my apartment two years ago, I was told that he lived there, in the old brownstone row house on the corner. The weather the week before our encounter had been unusually warm and bright, but, on the Saturday we met, it had suddenly turned gray and cold. My mood matched the day. Part of the blues came from feeling particularly unprepared and uninspired for preaching on Sunday. Late in the afternoon, a local store called to say an order I had left was ready to be picked up. My initial response was that it could wait until Monday. About half an hour later, something made me decide to just go pick up my stuff before the shop closed. It was only a ten-minute walk downtown. The fresh air would be good for me.

Heading down the busy street, I noticed a man standing on the front stoop of the rabbi's house.

On the return trip, about twenty minutes later, the man was still there. I approached him and asked, "You wouldn't happen to be the rabbi, would you?"

He responded with a tentative "Y-e-s."

"Hello" I said, extending my hand. "My name is Klara. I live next door and have been meaning to come and meet you."

"Well" he replied, "I have been standing here waiting for someone to come who could help me with something."

"What is it you need help with, Rabbi?"

"I need someone to turn up my thermostat."

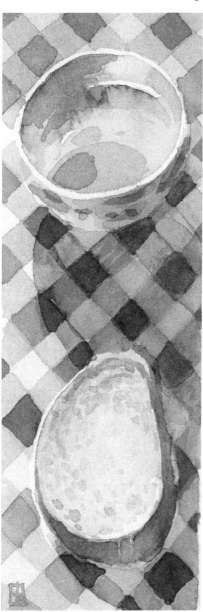

It was a bit puzzling, but I offered, "I think I could help you with that, Rabbi."

Upon entering the house, I saw a group of four or five men around a table, books open in front of them. Each had a yarmulke on his head. They stood in greeting. The answer to the puzzle dawned on me: Saturday … Sabbath … no work.

"Ahhh, Rabbi! It is your Sabbath, isn't it?" I exclaimed.

He smiled and nodded, then showed me the thermostat. I adjusted it from about fifty-five degrees to seventy. Upon leaving the house, the rabbi, with a sparkle in his eyes, exclaimed, "Amazing, simply amazing!"

"What is amazing, Rabbi?" I asked.

"Well…" he said, "You just happened to walk by!"

As I left the rabbi's house, the steeple bells of the large Catholic church across the street began to call the faithful to Mass. I paused to listen to the chimes. Another one of my neighbors, Mary Jane, is a member of that church. Attending daily Mass there has been her discipline for fifty years. At 7:00 each morning, the church bells call Mary Jane to Mass. They also mark the end of my morning meditation and prayer.

At home, I took another look at the scriptures for Sunday, this time reading before and after the lectionary text. Preceding the appointed passage, was the story of Jesus and the disciples being chastised on the Sabbath for plucking grains of wheat. Jesus duly chastises them back.

Sabbath … What was it about? Perhaps Sabbath meant suspending yourself in that something which was greater than yourself, and joyfully and restfully abiding with God and each other, just like the rabbi and Mary Jane. *There* was my sermon. "Yes, Rabbi" I thought, "God is simply amazing!"

A Gift of Baptism

— by Edmond Browning

ONE OF THE MOST powerful experiences of my twelve years in Japan happened on the island of Yaeyama. It is a small island halfway between Okinawa and Taiwan. There was a small group of Christians on the island, but no church or regular priestly presence there. I had been asked by the bishop to go and see about establishing a church on Yaeyama. Accompanying me was a young Okinawan priest and an elderly Okinawan deacon. On our flight over from Okinawa, the deacon told me about a young man named Higa San who lived on Yaeyama. The story I heard of Higa San's Christian journey was so remarkable that I asked the deacon to call Higa San and invite him to dinner that evening. During dinner, Higa San shared his pilgrimage. In his early teens he had contracted leprosy. When the disease was discovered, most of his friends and relatives rejected him. He was sent away to the leper colony on Airakuen, which is a small island near enough to Okinawa to be connected by a small bridge. Upon arriving at the colony, Higa San was further devastated by the distorted faces and hands and feet of the other lepers. He did not know how he was going to endure his new life.

Over the first year, the leper community reached out to him in an incredible way, so much so that he said he had never felt such warmth and acceptance. They invited him into their community, but, more importantly, into their hearts. He began to go to the church in the leper colony. The church community there was an Episcopal congregation of over 700 persons. It had been established by a man named Aoki, himself a leper, and two American priests serving on Okinawa. The members of the colony called their church simply The House of Prayer. It was through the love and support of the lepers who worshiped with him in The House of Prayer that Higa San began to understand the real strength and real purpose of community. Out of this understanding naturally developed Higa San's personal relationship with his Lord. And so he was baptized and began to receive Eucharist regularly, thanks to the continuing visits of Okinawan priests. After several years his leprosy was arrested, and he was given permission to leave the leper colony and return home to Yaeyama.

His testimony that evening was as moving as anything I have ever heard. As we parted that night, I invited him to join the three of us at eight o'clock the next morning for Eucharist.

The next day, even before the sun had risen, the telephone rang in our room. A voice eagerly said, "I am here!" to which I responded, "Who is this?"

"Higa," was the reply.

"Higa? What time is it?" I asked.

It was five-thirty! Since he was the only one who was joining us, I invited him to come on up to the room and said that we would have Eucharist. While we were picking up our bedding off the tatami mats, and I was preparing for the Eucharist, I could not help but ask, "Higa, why have you come so early?"

He replied, "When I went home, I could not sleep. I wrestled all night thinking about meeting my Lord in the bread and wine of the Eucharist." As we listened to Higa San explain his strange behavior, we realized that, without an established church or priest on Yaeyama, he had not received the Eucharist in two years. "And so," Higa San concluded, "I told myself, 'you do not need to wait any longer—go to the hotel now.'"

At six, as the sun rose, and we broke bread together, we all felt God's presence as never before. There, on an island that most Americans have never heard of, from a young man known only to his few friends on that island, we saw the faith of the Apostles, a faith of expectancy.

For Small Group Discussion

Share your earliest memory of being formed in faith.

What was it in the experience that leads you to name it as formational for you?

What changes did the experience bring to your life?

Pass the loaf of bread around the circle, each person taking a piece. As you eat it, recall a memorable experience of worship or a memory of a special meal at home with families and friends. Share your memories with another person.

When have you felt you were strongly abiding in God through a community of faith?

When did you feel included? Or excluded? Why?

Describe an encounter with someone, through which you came to know God more deeply. Describe a time when you felt estranged from God or from a community of faith.

What was the cause?

Was the relationship with God and/or the community restored?

If so, how? If not, why not?

Reflecting

Scripture

Exodus 20:8–11   Remember the Sabbath
(also Deuteronomy 5:12–15)

Deuteronomy 6:4–9   Teach your children

1 Kings 3:6–14   Solomon's prayer for wisdom

Psalm 78:1–8   Give ear to God's words and teach them

Matthew 6:5–15   The Lord's Prayer
(also Luke 11:1–4)

Matthew 12:1–8   On keeping the Sabbath
(also Mark 2: 23–28; Luke 6:1–5)

Matthew 26:26–29 The Lord's Supper
(also Mark 14:22–25; Luke 22:14–20; 1 Corinthians 11:23–26)

Luke 10:38–42   Jesus visits Mary and Martha

Luke 24:13–35   The walk to Emmaus

John 6:1–15   Feeding the five thousand
(also Matthew 14:13–21; Mark 6:30–44; Luke 9:10–17; and feeding of four thousand in Mark 8:1–10 and Matthew 15:32–29)

John 17:1–26   Jesus prays for the church

Acts 2:41–47   Life among the believers

1 Corinthians 12:12–30
                     One body with many members

Ephesians 3:14–21 Paul's prayer for the Ephesians

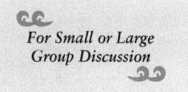

For Small or Large Group Discussion

Refer to the scripture selections.
   Choose one or two that speak to you, and discuss them.

What word or phrase jumps out at you?

What does the passage say to you?

What is it calling you to do?

Consider any of the suggested hymns that relate to your conversation.
   Read over the Prayer Book selections.

What light do they shed on your conversation?

Hymns

The Hymnal 1982

> I come with joy to meet my Lord, #304
> Come, risen Lord, #305
> Let us break bread together, #325
> Now the silence, #333
> For the bread which you have broken,
>   #340, #341
> Ubi caritas, #577, #581, #606
> How firm a foundation, #637
> *(see other hymns, "Holy Eucharist" section,*
> *The Hymnal 1982, #300–347)*
> Psalm 23, #646, #663, #664
> The Lord's Prayer, #674

Wonder, Love, and Praise

> All who hunger gladly gather, #760
> As we gather at your table, #763
> Taste and see, #764
> O Lord hear my prayer, #827
> Ubi caritas, #831
> The Lord's Prayer, #833
> Fraction anthems, #875–877

Lift Every Voice and Sing II

> Break thou the bread of life, #146
> I'm a-going to eat at the
>   welcome table, #148

The Book of Common Prayer

Collect for Proper 28, p. 236
Prayers for the Church, pp. 816–817
The Catechism:
> The Church, pp. 854–855
> Prayer and Worship, p. 856
> The Holy Eucharist, p. 859

Eucharistic Prayers, pp. 333, 361, 367, 369, 372
> *(see also* Enriching Our Worship 1, *pp. 57–65)*

Postcommunion Prayers, pp. 339, 365–366
> *(see also* Enriching Our Worship 1, *pp. 69–70)*

For Small or Large Group Discussion

Think about how, when, and where you are most likely to learn something about God.

Where is it that you feel closest to God?

What have you learned most recently about God?

Is there a particular book or study program that led to a new awakening in faith for you?

Think of the community to which you feel most connected.

What led you there?

Why do you stay?

In your community, how do you feed each other?

How do you share the love of Christ with each other?

Describe your prayer life.

How often do you pray, and when?

How do you pray?

What is your favorite place to pray?

Do you have a prayer partner or group?

Do you have a spiritual partner?

Look at some prayers in scripture (1 Kings 8:22–61; 2 Kings 19:15–20; 1 Chronicles 29:10–19; Jeremiah 32:16–24; Daniel 9:3–19; Jonah 2:1–9; Luke 18:9–14; Acts 4:24–31).

How might these prayers inform your own?

Read about the principal kinds of prayer—adoration, praise, thanksgiving, penitence—as outlined in the Catechism, the Book of Common Prayer, pp. 856–857.

Which of the principal kinds of prayer do you pray most often?

Which do you seldom use?

If you have a favorite prayer—either from the Prayer Book or from any other book of prayer—share it with the group.

What is this prayer's origin?

The vow to continue in the apostles' teaching and fellowship comes straight from scripture (Acts 2:42) and describes the immediate response of those who had just been baptized at Pentecost. The following verses summarize the resulting life pattern of those early Christians in Jerusalem. Their life together included awe, wonders, and signs; believing together; having things in common; the selling of possessions and the distribution of proceeds to the needy; having good will; much time spent in the temple and breaking of bread at home; and glad and generous hearts and much praising of God. Because of all these aspects of their community, many were added to their numbers.

How do we measure up? For many people today, engagement in the apostles' teaching is limited. Time in fellowship is an exception to the norm. Worship for many (if it happens at all) is most often only in church, and prayer only at meals or in times of crisis. In comparison, the pattern of the Early Church sounds very different. How might we recapture the sense that our learning together, our fellowship, our worship, and our prayer are things that we can't help but do? How can baptism again become something in which we immerse ourselves, so that the first things we do in response to it are to learn and share and worship and pray?

Tom Groome, a Roman Catholic professor of religious education, tells a story of taking a taxicab from the airport in Chicago, with a Jewish cab driver. On the ride into town, they entered into an interesting theological conversation. As Tom left the cab, the driver said to him, "You know, the problem with you Christians is that you have taken your worship out of the home."

The cab driver has a good point. Have we mistakenly isolated our teaching and fellowship, our breaking of bread and prayers primarily to church, on one or two hours a Sunday? Can we somehow make our baptismal response more a part of our daily life—beginning with this vow?

Reflectively read one or two of the following quotes.
What is your response?

As I was nearing the end of the evangelization of the first six Masai communities, I began looking towards baptism. So I went to the old man Ndangoya's community to prepare them for the final step.

I told them I had finished the imparting of the Christian message inasmuch as I could. I had taught them everything I knew about Christianity. Now it was up to them. They could reject it or accept it. I could do no more. If they did accept it, of course, it required public baptism. So I would go away for a week or so and give them the opportunity to make their judgment on the gospel of Jesus Christ. If they did accept it, then there would be baptism. However, baptism wasn't automatic. Over the course of the year it had taken me to instruct them, I had gotten to know them very well indeed.

So I stood in front of the assembled community and began: "This old man sitting here has missed too many of our instruction meetings. He was always out herding cattle. He will not be baptized with the rest. These two on the side will be baptized because they always attended, and understood very well what we talked about. So did this young mother. She will be baptized. But that man there has obviously not understood the instructions. And that lady there has scarcely believed the gospel message. They cannot be baptized. And this warrior has not shown enough effort...."

The old man, Ndangoya, stopped me politely but firmly, "Padri, why are you trying to break us up and separate us? During this whole year that you have been teaching us, we have talked about these things when you were not here, at night around the fire. Yes, there have been lazy ones in this community, but they have been helped by those with much energy. There are stupid ones in the community, but they have been helped by those who are intelligent. Yes, there are ones with little faith in this village, but they have been helped by those with much faith. Would you turn out and drive off the lazy ones and the ones with little faith and the stupid ones? From the first day I have spoken for these people. And I speak for them now. Now, on this day one year later, I can declare for them and for all this community, that we have reached the step in our lives where we can say, 'We believe.'"

— Vincent Donovan, from *Christianity Rediscovered*,
as quoted in *A Sourcebook about Liturgy*, Liturgy
Training Publications, pp. 18–19

Uyai Mose

Uyai mose, tinamate mwari (x3)
Uyai mose zvino

Come all you people, come praise
your maker (x3)
Come now and worship the Lord
— A well-known hymn from Zimbabwe
in the Shona language

Blessed Lord, who cause all holy Scriptures to be written for our learning: Grant us so to hear them, read, mark, learn and inwardly digest them, that we may embrace and ever hold fast the blessed hope of everlasting life, which you have given us in our Savior Jesus Christ; who lives and reigns with you and the Holy Spirit, one God, for ever and ever. Amen.

— Proper 28, BCP, p. 236

"To teach is to create a space in which the community of truth is practiced."
"Truth is an eternal conversation about things that matter, conducted with passion and discipline."

— Parker Palmer "Good Teaching: A Matter of Living the Mystery" *Change Magazine*, Jan/Feb 1990. http://couragerenewal.org/parker/writings/good-teaching/

Hamotzi – Jewish blessing over bread

Baruch atah Adonai eloheinu Melech ha-aloom
ha-motz lechem min ha-aretz.
Blessed are You, O God, Ruler of the Universe, who brings forth bread from the earth.

Day by day, dear Lord,
of thee three things I pray:
to see thee more clearly,
love thee more dearly,
follow thee more nearly,
day by day.

— Prayer of Richard of Chichester,
The Hymnal 1982, # 654

Let us break bread together on our knees

Let us break bread together on our knees;
Let us drink wine together on our knees;
Let us praise God together on our knees;
When I fall on my knees, with my face to the rising sun,
O Lord have mercy on me.

— Afro-American spiritual, *The Hymnal 1982*, #325

Before the missionaries came, my people used to sit outside their temples for a long time meditating and preparing themselves before entering. Then they would virtually creep to the altar to offer their petition and afterwards would again sit a long time outside, this time to "breathe life" into their prayers. The Christians, when they came, just got up, uttered a few sentences, said Amen, and were done. For that reason my people called them haoles, "without breath," or those who failed to breathe life into their prayers.

— Mother Alice Kaholusauna (quoted in *Walking on Water: Reflections on Faith and Art*, Madeline L'Engle)

Lord,
To those who hunger, give bread.
And to those who have bread
Give them a hunger for justice.

— A Nicaraguan prayer,
source unknown

A Blessing Over Bread

Blessed are you, O Lord our God;
you bring forth bread from the earth
and make the risen Lord to be for us the Bread of life;
Grant that we who daily seek the bread which sustains
    our bodies
may also hunger for the food of everlasting life,
Jesus Christ our Lord. Amen.

— "Agapé for Maundy Thursday,"
The Book of Occasional Services

Unleavened Bread for Eucharist

4 3/4 cup whole wheat flour
1 egg yolk
1/2 cup plus 1 Tbsp. honey
7 tbs. olive oil (1/2 cup less 1 tbs.)
1 1/8 cup lukewarm water
pinch of salt

Add egg yolk to flour; then add oil, honey, and salt. Mix well.

Slowly add water (more water may be added if necessary; dough should not be too wet or too dry.)

Flatten the dough into patties 4 inches in diameter and about 1/4-inch thick.

Cut a cross into the center of each round of bread, using a knife.

Bake on an ungreased cookie sheet at 350 degrees until golden brown, about 10–20 minutes.

Yield: Approximately 10 loaves. Each round is enough for 20–25 people. Can be frozen for later use.

Remember the Sabbath,
and keep it holy.

— Exodus 20; Deuteronomy 5

Re-member the Sabbath,
and keep it wholly.

— inspired by Don Postema

"Remembering the Sabbath" means "Remember that everything you have received is a blessing. Remember to delight in your life, in the fruits of your labor. Remember to stop and offer thanks for the wonder of it." *Remember,* as if we would forget. Indeed, the assumption is that we will forget. And history has proven that, given enough time, we will.

"Remember the Sabbath" is not simply a life-style suggestion. It is a spiritual precept in most of the world's spiritual traditions—ethical precepts that include prohibitions against killing, stealing, and lying. How can forgetting the Sabbath possibly be morally and socially dangerous? How can forgetting to be restful, sing songs, and take delight in creation be as reprehensible as murder, robbery, and deceit?

It was not Israel that kept the Sabbath, it is said, but the Sabbath kept Israel.

— Wayne Muller in *Sabbath: Restoring the Sacred Rhythm of Rest,* pp. 6–7, 9

Be still and know that I am God.
Be still and know that I am.
Be still and know.
Be still.
Be.

— Don Postema in
Catch Your Breath, p. 19

The radical (from radix or "root") of the words "pray" or "prayer" is common to many words relating to the sacred. In fact, when this radical is substituted for the standing-person radical in the word for "believe" in pronouns, the English "you" or "he" becomes the God-directed "Thou" or "He," without connotation of gender. The Chinese solved the question of a gender-neutral God-language long before Christianity arrived in China.

Responding

Practicing Together:

- When do you take Sabbath time with God? If you have a regular practice of community worship, describe it. How has it changed over the years? As a resource, read and discuss Don Postema's *Catch Your Breath*.

- In what way are "The Prayers of the People" prayed in your church? What is expressed by how you pray together? Is time given to prayer outside of Sunday worship service, at meetings or classes? How might you integrate prayer more fully into the teaching, fellowship, and general life of the community?

- Arrange for your group to write the Prayers of the People for use in a Sunday worship service. For guidance, review the rubrics and forms of the prayers found in the Prayer Book (pp. 383–393), and the questions about prayer in the Catechism (pp. 856–857).

- What do you like about how your community worships together? What do you not like? What do think might be changed to make it more inclusive of everyone?

- Bake unleavened bread together using the recipe in the Reflecting section. Arrange for it to be used in a regular service of Eucharist at your church. Or, cook a simple meal together and share it.

- Read Psalms of praise or thanksgiving (Psalms 95, 100). As a group, write one together. Do so by folding the paper down after each added sentence so that each writer sees only the sentence immediately before his or her own. Pray the new psalm together.

- Ask someone in the group to volunteer to lie down on a large piece of mural paper while another volunteer from the group traces a body outline around him/her. When the outlining is completed, ask the others to gather around it. Read 1 Corinthians 12. Invite each person to stand on the part of the body that they feel most called to be, and speak their reason. For example: "I stand on the mouth because I feel called to be the voice for those who have no voice." If possible, participants should remain in place together on the outline of the body. (If participants are uncomfortable standing together, have them write their phrase on the outline of the body, in the place they identify; then all stand in a circle around the figure.) When everyone has taken a place, sing the familiar song, "We are one in the Spirit, we are one in the Lord," or the fraction hymn used as the Gathering song, or some other song of your choice that evokes the image of one body. This exercise could be incorporated into the closing prayer of the session.

- What kinds of adult religious education take place in your church? How many people participate? What are some creative ways you might encourage faith formation for adults? As a resource, read and discuss *Fashion Me a People,* by Maria Harris.

Practicing at Home:

- Bake bread with someone and eat it together. Or visit a good local bakery. Talk to the bakers about their art. Enjoy the smells. Buy a fresh loaf to take home for a meal.

- Invite friends over for a meal. Begin the meal with the opening words of The Great Thanksgiving from the Book of Common Prayer (p. 361), then invite everyone to speak their thanksgivings. Keep a list of all the things for which you give thanks.

- Take note of how you live the apostles' teaching and fellowship, the breaking of bread and the prayers—Monday through Saturday. What else might you do?

- Make a plan for a Sabbath day of rest for yourself. Put it on the calendar. On that day, record the feelings of the day in your journal. If you simply cannot manage a day, build small times of rest into each day.

- Is scripture study part of your regular practice? Do you participate in any form of Christian education? If no, plan a manageable daily or weekly discipline of scripture reading. Or read a short spiritual classic.

- Find ways to incorporate prayer more fully in your life. A familiar discipline is known as "breath prayer." It is a very short (usually one sentence) and is prayed in a meditative and repetitive way, regulated by breathing. The most familiar, traditional breath prayer is the "Jesus Prayer": "Lord Jesus Christ (while breathing in), have mercy on me, a sinner (while breathing out)." A way to help start the habit is to put a small colored sticker in places you regularly glance at, such as on your bathroom mirror, or the kitchen faucet, or your wallet, or rear-view mirror. Say that brief prayer every time you see a dot. Another similar well-known prayer form is Centering Prayer, which, when your mind wanders, uses a sacred word to draw attention back to God and the moment.

For inspiration you might read these classic books: Practicing the Presence of God (Brother Lawrence), *The Way of the Pilgrim, Cloud of Unknowing, Testament of Devotion* (Thomas Kelly).

Closing Prayer

Sing again the Opening Song, "The disciples knew the Lord Jesus," which was sung in the time of Gathering.
Take a moment to share thanksgivings and personal prayer needs.
Close with the following prayer and blessing.

O God the Father of our Lord Jesus Christ, our only Savior, the Prince of Peace: Give us grace seriously to lay to heart the great dangers we are in by our unhappy divisions; take away all hatred and prejudice, and whatever else may hinder us from godly union and concord; that, as there is but one Body and one Spirit, one hope of our calling, one Lord, one Faith, one Baptism, one God and Father of all, so we may be all of one heart and of one soul, united in one holy bond of truth and peace, of faith and charity, and may with one mind and one mouth glorify you; through Jesus Christ our Lord. Amen.

— "For the Unity of the Church," The Book of Common Prayer, p. 818

Everlasting Father, we your gathered people are your Church, for without us the Church has no reality: Guide us as we seek to discover the gifts you have given each of us that we might minister to others in your name; through Jesus Christ, our Savior, the light of the world. Amen.

— Elizabeth Rankin Geitz, *Women's Uncommon Prayers*, p. 313

August 1

I go back every few days to check on the loon family. Found a small cove where I can sit and watch. It is sheltered and hidden, the water is calm, good for picture taking. I could hear the adults gently talking to the little one, and see them feed it. Peter came out yesterday. We went over to Woodbury Pond, all the way to the end of that lake, about five miles roundtrip. It was an eerie, misty morning. On the way we passed two loon families, one family at each end of the lake, each with two chicks. Against the white mist, you could really see them.

Session Four

Will you persevere in resisting evil, and, whenever you fall into sin, repent and return to the Lord?

Gathering

Place a rough wooden or pottery dish next to the bowl of water.
Fill it with shards of sea/beach glass of various colors. (Bags of colored sea glass can be purchased at craft stores.)
Have enough sea glass for a handful for each person.

OPENING SONG: De Noche

Sing this slowly, and repeatedly.

If good singers are present, have them sing in four-part harmony.

This song comes from the Taizé Community in France.
Taizé music is easily available in a Google search or from
GIA Publications (www.giamusic.com). There is also a
Taizé Community website (Taize.fr).

De noche iremos, de noche
    que para encontrar la fuente,
    Sólo la sed nos alumbra,
    Sólo la sed nos alumbra.

By night we hasten in darkness,
    to search for the living water,
    only our thirst leads us onward,
    only our thirst leads us onward.
                 — *Songs from Taizé*, #12

Other options from Taizé:
    Stay with us Blood Jesus Christ
    Dont be afraid

MARK 4:35–41   Jesus Calms the Storm

During the reading of this passage—on cue when the reader says,
"A great windstorm arose"—have participants create the sound of a storm, beginning quietly with drumming of
fingers, then clapping, then stomping. End the noise-making suddenly with "Peace! Be still!"

On that day, when evening had come, he said to them,
> "Let us go across to the other side."

And leaving the crowd behind,
> they took him with them in the boat, just as he was.

Other boats were with him.

A great windstorm arose,
> and the waves beat into the boat,
> so that the boat was already being swamped.

But he was in the stern, asleep on a cushion;
> and they woke him up and said to him,
> "Teacher, do you not care
> that we are perishing?"

He woke up and rebuked the wind,
> and said to the sea,
> "Peace! Be still!"

Then the wind ceased,
> and there was a dead calm.

He said to them,
> "Why are you afraid?
> Have you still no faith?"

And they were filled with great awe
> and said to one another.
> "Who is this, that even the wind
> and the sea obey him?

Psalm 69:1–3, 12–18

Use the words "Save me, O God" as an antiphon; proclaim it at the beginning and at the end of each section.

Save me, O God,
  for the waters have risen up to my neck.
I am sinking in deep mire,
  and there is no firm ground for my feet.
I have come into deep waters,
  and the torrent washes over me.
I have grown weary with my crying;
    my throat is inflamed;
    my eyes have failed from looking for my God.

Zeal for your house has eaten me up;
  the scorn of those who scorn you has fallen upon me.
I humbled myself with fasting,
  but that was turned to my reproach.
I put on sack-cloth also,
  and became a byword among them.
Those who sit at the gate murmur against me,
  and the drunkards make songs about me.

But as for me, this is my prayer to you,
  at the time you have set, O Lord:
"In your great mercy, O God,
  answer me with your unfailing help.
Save me from the mire; do not let me sink;
  let me be rescued from those who hate me
  and out of the deep waters.
Let not the torrent of waters wash over me,
  neither let the deep swallow me up;
  do not let the Pit shut its mouth upon me.
Answer me, O Lord, for your love is kind;
  in your great compassion, turn to me."

For Personal, Silent Reflection

Imagine being in the boat with Jesus and the disciples. You do not know how to swim, and you are terrified you will sink. Jesus does not seem to be frightened; he is fast asleep on a cushion. You frantically wake him. Spend a few moments in silence wondering about the following:

What do you expect Jesus to do?

What do you think when he calms the sea?

Jesus asks, "Why are you afraid? Have you no faith?"

What are the things you are afraid of?

What have you already seen of the power of God?

What do these evidences of God's power tell you about how to proceed?

Think of a time when you felt overwhelmed.

How did you cry out to God? What happened?

The Lord's Prayer

Sing this prayer using The Hymnal 1982 *setting, #674.*

"Forgive our sins as we forgive"
    you taught us, Lord, to pray;
but you alone can grant us grace
    to live the words we say.

How can your pardon reach and bless
    the unforgiving heart
that broods on wrongs and will not let
    old bitterness depart?

In blazing light your cross reveals
    the truth we dimly knew,
how small the debts [men owe] to us, [are owed]
    how great our debt to you.

Lord, cleanse the depths within our souls,
    and bid resentment cease;
then, reconciled to God [and man,] [and all]
    our lives will spread your peace.
          — Rosamond E. Herklots, *The Hymnal 1982*, #674

Collect

O God, by whom the meek are guided in judgment,
and light rises up in darkness for the godly:
Grant us, in all our doubts and uncertainties,
the grace to ask what you would have us to do,
that the Spirit of wisdom may save us from all false choices,
and that in your light we may see light,
and in your straight path may not stumble;
through Jesus Christ our Lord. Amen.
          —"For Guidance," The Book of Common Prayer, p. 832

Sharing

IN OHIO, where I grew up, summer storms were vicious. In that flat landscape, they would appear out of nowhere in what seemed an instant, bringing wild winds, torrential rains or hail, blinding lightning, and thunder that shook the earth. Our house was on the lower side of a hill. When it rained, water would pour into our garage. We would dig ditches, trying to redirect the water around the foundation and away from the house, but our ditches were always quickly washed away.

During one particularly harsh storm—with the garage flooding—Mom ran out to re-dig the trench. I went with her to lend moral support and sat inside the garage, watching. She was in the doorway of the garage, standing in a large puddle with a metal hoe in her hand, when the huge oak tree—which was right next to the garage and also very close to the vantage point I had chosen—suddenly exploded. Of the two of us, Mom was closer to the exploding tree, and the strike was headed for her. The lightning was so bright and so loud that I remember not being able to see or hear anything after it ... and the air felt very funny.

Mom scooped me up and ran inside. Enfolded in her loving arms as she landed both of us in the large wing chair in the living room, I wailed "I don't know who did this, God or Jesus, but I wish they would not do it any more!" I was about four years old at the time. It is one of my earliest memories. To this day, I jump at a thunderclap. If I'm speaking when the thunder occurs, my voice cracks. As a child, I simply wanted to know the cause of the bad thing that had happened, and wanted it to go away. As an adult, I am left with a memory that provides an instinctual link to fear, to knowing something is wrong. Whenever faced with evil, I feel—rising from somewhere deep within my soul—the sensation of being shaken by a thunderclap.

THE TRIENNIAL General Convention of the Episcopal Church in 1991 was held in Phoenix, Arizona. Three decades after the civil rights movement, the issue at hand was that due to the governor's veto, Arizona would not recognize the Martin Luther King Jr. holiday as a paid holiday, despite a vote in the affirmative. Before the convention, there was much debate about the location, and whether or not the Episcopal Church should boycott the city and move the convention elsewhere, as did the National Football League in moving the Super Bowl from Phoenix to Los Angeles. I was present at the Convention as volunteer staff. As print officer, I had a close-up view of legislation going to both the House of Deputies and House of Bishops.

The decision was made to keep the General Convention in Phoenix, but while there we were to do all we could to raise awareness about racism. During the two weeks, a good deal of soul-searching was done, information was gathered, and an anti-racism resolution was passed. We heard speeches about racism and participated in daily roundtables consisting of Bible study, prayer, and discussion. Everyone did a "racism audit," which was a process of thinking formally and systemically think about issues in an attempt to uncover anything done or left undone that might constitute racism in our lives, either personally or institutionally.

By action of Convention, the Martin Luther King Jr. Legacy Scholarship Fund was begun to provide support for young people attending one of the three historically Black colleges. Provisions also were made to assist Native American and Asian American students. Finally, commitments were formed to continue the examination process back home, including doing "racism audits" at the diocesan level. We were hopeful that we had made a difference, that what we had done in Phoenix would bring about change.

At the convention's closing Eucharist, we were all seated at tables of eight to ten people, where we had been for the daily morning roundtables. At the Great Thanksgiving, I looked over my shoulder at the large group of clergy waiting to bring the bread and wine to each table. This was about twelve years after the Episcopal Church had opened ordination to women. Startled by what I saw, I spontaneously whispered with exasperation to my neighbor, "Oh my, they are all men!" To which she, an African American woman, replied, "Yes, and they are all white."

Suddenly, my own racism smacked me in the face… I was stunned! Yes, they were all men… BUT yes indeed, they were all white… Hidden in plain sight, I had only noticed half the problem even after two weeks of focusing on racism. I felt embarrassed and quietly wept through communion. "O Lord, open my eyes that I may see!"

Between then and now, I have participated in more anti-racism trainings than I can count. Yet, another three decades have passed and tears still flow… In listening to the memorial service for Representative John Lewis and in reading his letter to us as a nation, penned just before he died; in watching the news about the murders of Black people by whites as if it were still Jim Crow, and of trials that acquit the murderers; when because of COVID, I at sixty-five and not yet vaccinated didn't dare march for Black Lives Matter but watched and heard the protests go by from my porch; during a multi-racial public reading sponsored by the Maine Council of Churches during the pandemic on Zoom, for the Martin Luther King Jr. Memorial Day; watching the video on NPR of the descendants of Frederick Douglass reading his reflections about the Fourth of July from the view point of slaves.

For centuries, racism has been so ingrained in our psyches, that unconsciously, like me, we look, but just do not see. Only now are we beginning to think deeply about what the Civil War symbols that we so proudly displayed, have said to people of color and only now we are taking down the statues and flags and renaming buildings. Murders and accusations continue to be inflicted on our Black and Brown brothers and sisters while their incarceration rates skyrocket. We continue a failed war on drugs rather than dealing with root causes of poverty, racism, mental illness and other injustices.

Only now do we offer verbal acknowledgments for land stolen from Indigenous peoples, and change Columbus Day to Indigenous People's Day, yet they still must fight for their rights to land, healthcare, and recognition while we argue about reparations. Thousands of migrants and refugees are political pawns at borders in our own country and around the globe.

The institutional systems of oppression and white privilege remain largely in place. Efforts mount to end affirmative action, economic disparities grow, and the lives of public servants from marginalized populations, are regularly threatened. Equal representation is a long way off—even in the Church.

With social media however, while harsh voices are amplified, we also can no longer easily avoid seeing the realities. They come to us immediately rather than in newspapers, weeks, days or months later (if at all), now backed up by body cameras and cell phone videos. Maybe, just maybe, are we finally be at a tipping point?

Setting the evils of racism right has been like slowly peeling back an onion, one layer at a time. Sometimes it will, and should make us weep in lament and contrition, especially those of us who have benefitted from the status quo. May this time finally bring deep, positive change and renewed life for us all.

Smoking

— by Alice Jellema

SOME PEOPLE CAN smoke cigarettes just at parties. I cannot. I started smoking in January 1976. By 1986 I had tried to stop many times. Each failure increased my shame and despair, and those feelings only strengthened the addiction. I could not quit. I knew that nicotine was bad for me, but it had all the power. I was a smoker.

One night I was wakened by an unusual noise. It was my normally gentle cat—made strange by darkness and her unusual level of excitement. She was making a fierce sound as she toyed with a tiny mouse. The mouse tried to run: the cat pounced and trapped it. The mouse tried to hide: the cat found it. In desperation the mouse sat back on its hind legs and boxed at the cat: the cat continued her game.

All of a sudden, I felt like I was the (powerless) mouse, and cigarettes were like the cat. Determining to take a less powerless and more godlike role, I slapped the floor and turned on the light, startling the cat enough for the mouse to escape. Then I went and put my cigarettes in a jar of water in the kitchen and went back to sleep.

The next three months were very hard. Then for a few years it was only moderately hard. I still sometimes dream, joylessly, about cigarettes. But I have not smoked since November 17, 1986. I can't explain how, except that God is more powerful than nicotine. I am no longer a smoker. I am free.

For Small Group Discussion

As you break into small groups, go to the bowl in the center of the room and take a small handful of sea glass. As you hold the sea glass, think about what "evil" means to you. Think about the forms of evil with which you are most familiar in your life.

Talk about a time when you became aware that something you were doing (or not doing) was causing evil; if the specifics you recall are potentially embarrassing or harmful to yourself or others, give a broader, more general outline of the situation.

What made you recognize and name this evil?

What brought the evil to your awareness?

How did you respond when you became aware of the evil?

Did you pray? If so, what was your prayer?

Did the experience change your definition of evil?

Feel the smooth edges of your handful of sea glass. Remember a time when you resisted evil, and name that evil.

What was the hardest part of resisting the evil?

What helped you to resist?

What was the result for you?

How was the gathered community of help to you?

Spend a few moments in silence thinking about the situations you have described. How was God working in you and in the situation? As you return to the large group, prayerfully place your shards of glass in the bowl of water.

Reflecting

Scripture

Genesis 2:9	The tree of good and evil
Genesis 3	The first sin
Genesis 4:1–16	Cain murders Abel
Genesis 4:23–24	Lamech kills a man
Genesis 6–9	Noah and the flood
Genesis 22:1–19	Binding of Isaac
Psalm 51	Prayer for cleansing and pardon
Psalm 107, Part 1	Thanksgiving for deliverance
Jonah (all chapters)	
Matthew 12:43–45	Return of unclean spirits
(also Luke 11:24–26)	
Matthew 13:24–30, 36–43	
	Good seed among weeds
Mathew 18:21–35	How often should I forgive?
	The unforgiving servant
Matthew 26:69–75	Peter's denial of Jesus
(also Mark 14:66–72; Luke 22:54–62; John 18:15–18, 25–27)	
Matthew 27:3–10	Death of Judas
Mark 1:21–28	Man with the unclean spirits
(also Luke 4:31–37)	
Mark 2:13–17	Jesus eats with tax collector
(also Matthew 9:9–13; Luke 5:27–32)	
Mark 5:1–20	Gerasene demoniac
(also Matthew 8:28–34; Luke 8:26–39)	
Mark 9:42–50	On temptation and sin
(also Matthew 18:6–9; Luke 17:1–2)	
Luke 4:1–13	The temptation of Jesus
(also Matthew 4:1–11)	

Luke 15:11–32	The prodigal and his brother
John 8:3–11	Woman caught in adultery
John 9	Healing blind man at pool of Siloam
Romans 6:1–4, 10–20	We who died to sin
Romans 7:14–25a	Paul's inner conflict
Romans 12:9–21	Overcome evil with good
1 Peter 3:9–12	Do not repay evil for evil
Revelation 20:1–3, 7–10	
	Satan bound in the final conflict

Hymns

The Hymnal 1982

Wilt thou forgive, #140, #141

From deepest woe I cry to thee, #151

There's a wideness in God's mercy, #469, #470

Breathe on me, Breath of God, #508

Lead us, heavenly Father, lead us, #559

O holy city, seen of John, #582, #583

Amazing grace! #671

A mighty fortress is our God, #687

Wonder, Love, and Praise

When from bondage we are summoned,
#753, #754

Lead me, guide me, along the way, #756

Heal me, hands of Jesus, #773

Lift Every Voice and Sing II

Come, thou fount of every blessing, #111

"An Evening Prayer"
(If I have wounded any soul today), #176

Amazing grace! #181

Love lifted me, #198

Stand by me, #200

There is a balm in Gilead, #203

Think of His goodness to you, #204

We'll understand it better by and by, #207

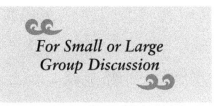

For Small or Large Group Discussion

Refer to the scripture selections. Choose one or two that speak to you, and discuss them.

What word or phrase jumps out at you?

What does the passage say to you?

What is it calling you to do?

Consider any of the suggested hymns that relate to your conversation.

Read over the Prayer Book selections and comments.

What light do they shed on your conversation?

The Book of Common Prayer

The Catechism, Sin and Redemption, p. 848
The Great Litany, pp. 148–155
Ash Wednesday, pp. 264–269
Collect for Ash Wednesday, p. 217
Collects for Lent, pp. 217–219
Baptismal vows of renunciation, p. 302
Penitential Orders, p. 319 (Rite I), p. 351 (Rite II)
Confessions, p. 331 (Rite I), p. 360 (Rite II)
Eucharistic Prayer A, pp. 361–366
The Reconciliation of a Penitent
    (Forms One and Two), pp. 447–452

The Book of Occasional Services

Preparation for Adults for Holy Baptism:
    Concerning the Catechumenate
    Admission of Catechumens
    During the Catechumenate
    Enrollment of Candidates for Baptism
    During Candidacy

Enriching Our Worship 1

Confession of Sin, p. 56

I remember a young father who, during a preparation class for his child's upcoming baptism, balked at the question about renunciation, the one that asks "Will you persevere against resisting evil and, whenever you sin, repent and return to the Lord?" He protested "O come on, we don't believe in that stuff anymore, do we?"

As the young father suggests, the concept of evil is not given careful consideration in American society. We reject the concept of evil entirely, as a superstitious holdover. We trivialize it by saying something is "sinfully good" or "wicked good." We project it onto others, as far away from ourselves as possible: the Soviet Union used to be the "evil empire," and now, in the early twenty-first century, there are "evil people" who are part of an "evil axis." Conversely, we can see evil almost as a commonplace, everyday explanation of anything that can cause offense, suffering, harm, disease—in short everything that is unpleasant. Someone once said that the devil has two main tricks: to convince us either that there is no evil or that everything is evil.

This Baptismal Covenant question has two clauses. The first asks us to "persevere" in resisting evil, all kinds of evil: that which we do to ourselves; that which we do to others; that which is inflicted upon us; that which is done to others on our behalf; things done and left undone. The assumption is that evil exists, inside each one of us and also outside—in others, in groups of others, and in the cosmos. The point of the first clause is that, regardless of whether evil is a personal shadow, or a corporate cloud, or a cosmic force, our goal is to recognize it and resolve over and over not be defeated by it.

The second part of the vow asks us to repent and return to the Lord when (not if) we sin. The assumption is that we will sin i.e., miss the mark. We are not perfect; we will make mistakes. We do not need to shoot for perfection. Our faith is one in which it is possible to get it wrong and still be faithful. We just need to keep trying to love, both ourselves and others. We are called to be more than merely lawful, and that calling is related to the measure Jesus used and always urged us to use: is what we do loving? Jesus was inviting us back to the root of Torah law—love of God and neighbor and self. Being faithful means that, when we are not loving, we repent and return and try again. In so doing, we grow, and transform both our relationships and the world.

For Small or Large Group Discussion

Name a time when some action or behavior that was expected of you and even deemed "lawful" by others did not seem to you like the right action or behavior. Spend some time contemplating the issues underneath this conflict. Try to avoid the "either/or" trap by asking yourself whether there might have been "right" aspects to both sides; whether there might have been a solution to this moral dilemma that built up, rather than tore down, the community; whether there is a loving response to the situation that will make the right action seem lawful and the lawful action seem right. Make a list of questions to ask yourself. Question all sides. Don't try to answer the questions or solve the overall problem; just write down your questions. Share the questions and any new insights that this approach has helped you to realize. Here are some sample questions:

What convinces me of my rightness?

What compels me to accommodate the views of those on the other side?

What are the roadblocks? What is actually possible?

Who has the most power in the situation?

How much power do I have to change things, and how can I use it effectively?

How can everyone win?

Have you ever witnessed an evil act that was a cause of harm to someone else?

Were you a party to the act? Or a bystander?

How did you feel at the time?

Did you intervene? If so, why and how? If not, why not?

What did you do immediately? Later?

What might Jesus have done in the situation?

What will you do if faced with a similar situation in the future?

Read the Confession of Sin in *Enriching Our Worship 1* (p. 56). Note the sentence: "We repent of the evil that enslaves us, the evil that we have done, and the evil done on our behalf." Name a situation in which you have felt some sense of guilt or complicity about an evil act committed by an organization to which you belong and, perhaps, support financially; or by your government, using your tax money; or by another government with which you have ties of heritage or ideology; or even by a church or faith to which you belong.

Did you resist? If so, how? What gave you the courage to resist?

Or did you look the other way? Why? What might help you to resist?

What emotions played a role in your response?

What scripture speaks to the situation?

When struggling with evil in your life or in the world:

How can you support others in persevering?

What role does confession play for you in repenting and returning?

What role does/might the church play?

What helps you to be an agent of transformation?

What helps the church to be an agent of transformation?

Reflectively read one or two of the following quotes.
What is your response?

Prayer for the Lady Who Forgave Us

There is a long suffering lady
with thin hands
who stands on the corner of Delphia and Lawrence
and forgives you.
"You are forgiven," she smiles.
The neighborhood is embarrassed.
It is sure it has done nothing wrong
yet everyday, in a small voice
it is forgiven.
On the way to the Jewel Food Store
housewives pass her with hard looks
they whisper in the cereal section.
Stan Dumke asked her right out
what she was up to
and she forgave him.
A group who care about the neighborhood
agree that if she was old it would be harmless
or if she was religious it would be understandable
but as it is ... they asked her to move on.
Like all things with eternal purposes
she stayed.
And she was informed upon.
On a most unforgiving day of snow and such
while she was reconciling a reluctant passerby
the State People
whose business is sanity,
persuaded her into a car.
She is gone.
We are reduced to forgetting.

> — J. Shea, *The Hour of the Unexpected*,
> as quoted in *Mighty Stories, Dangerous Rituals*
> by Herbert Anderson and Edward Foley, p. 175

The Prayer Before the Crucifix

All highest and glorious God,
Cast your light into the darkness
     of my heart.
Give me right faith,
    Firm hope,
    Perfect charity,
    And profound humility,
    With wisdom and perception,
O Lord, so that I may do what is
    truly your holy will.
Amen.

> — St. Francis

Through Baptism we say no to the world.
We declare that we no longer want to remain children of the darkness but we want to become children of the light, God's children. We do not want to escape the world, but we want to live in it without belonging to it. That is what baptism enables us to do.

— Henri Nouwen, *Bread for the Journey*

For baptism signifies that the old one and the sinful birth of flesh and blood are to be wholly drowned by the grace of God. We should therefore do justice to its meaning and make baptism a true and complete sign of the thing it signifies.

— Martin Luther, as quoted in *A Sourcebook about Liturgy*, Liturgy Training Publications, p. 11

A brother once sorrowfully asked Sisoes the Great: "Father, what can I do? I have fallen into sin." The Staretz answered him: "Rise again." The brother said: "I rose up and fell." The Staretz answered: "Rise again." The brother answered: "How often must I fall and rise up?" The Staretz said: "Until your death."

— Ignatius Byranchaninov, found in *Ordinary Graces*, p. 108

We shall have to repent in this generation, not so much for the evil deeds of the wicked people, but for the appalling silence of the good people.

— Martin Luther King Jr.

From the Lord's Prayer

Forgive us our sins
As we forgive those who sin against us.
Save us from the time of trial,
And deliver us from evil.

— The Book of Common Prayer, p. 364

In the hurts we absorb from one another, forgive us.
In times of temptation and test, strengthen us.
From trials too great to endure, spare us.
From the grip of all that is evil, free us.

— The New Zealand Prayer Book, p. 181

Loose the cord of mistakes binding us,
as we release the strands we hold
of others' guilt.
Don't let surface things delude us,
but free us from what holds us back.

— an Aramaic translation by Neil Douglas-Kotz
from *Prayers of the Cosmos: Meditations
on the Aramaic Words of Jesus*

Nine out of ten people start with the premise: "If I behave correctly I will one day see God clearly." Yet the biblical tradition is saying the exact opposite: If you see God clearly, you will behave in a good and human way. Your right behavior does not cumulatively lead to your true being; your true being leads to eventual right behavior. We almost all think that good morality will lead to mystical union, but, in fact, mystical union produces correct morality—along with a lot of joy left over. And the greatest surprise is that, sometimes, a bad moral response is the very collapsing of the ego that leads to our falling into the hands of the living God.

— Richard Rohr, *Hope Against
Darkness: the Transforming Vision of
St. Francis in an Age of Anxiety*, p. 30

Interview with Actor Lee Marvin:

How do I feel when I see myself on the screen? I found it very unpleasant recently when I saw a film of mine called *Point Blank*, which was a violent film. I remember; we made it for the violence. I was shocked at how violent it was. Of course, that was ten, fifteen, eighteen years ago. When I saw the film I literally almost could not stand up, I was so weak. I did *that*? I am capable of that kind of violence? See, *there* is the fright; and this is why I think guys back off eventually. They say, "No, I'm not going to put myself to those demons again." The demon being the self.

— from an interview at Salado, September 18, 1983,
in *Facing Evil*, Paul Woodruff and Harry Wilmer, eds.

That I feed the hungry, that I forgive an insult, that I love my enemy in the name of Christ— all these are undoubtedly great virtues. What I do unto the least of my brethren, that I do unto Christ. But what if I should discover that the least amongst them all, the poorest of all the beggars, the most impudent of all the offenders, the very enemy himself—that these are within me, and that I myself stand in need of the alms of my own kindness—that I myself am the enemy who must be loved? What then?

— C.G. Jung

Our deepest fear is not that we are inadequate.
Our deepest fear is that we are powerful beyond measure.
It is our light, not our darkness, that most frightens us.
We ask ourselves who am I to be brilliant, gorgeous,
        talented and fabulous?
Actually, who are you not to be?
You are a child of God!
Your playing small doesn't serve the world.
There's nothing enlightened about shrinking
        so that other people won't feel insecure around you.
We are born to make manifest the glory of God
        that is within us.
It is not just in some of us; it is in everyone.
As we let our own light shine, we unconsciously give other
        people permission to do the same
As we are liberated from our own fear,
        our presence automatically liberates others

— Nelson Mandela's 1994 Inauguration Speech

You've been fearful
of being absorbed in the ground
or drawn up by the air.

Now, your waterbead lets go
and drops into the ocean,
where it came from.

It no longer has the form it had,
but it's still water.
The essence is the same.

This giving up is not a repenting.
It's a deep honoring of yourself.

— Rumi

A Native American grandfather was talking to his grandson about how he felt about the tragedy on Sept 11th. He said, "I feel as if I have two wolves fighting in my heart. One wolf is the vengeful, angry, violent one. The other is the loving, compassionate one."

The grandson asked him, "Which wolf will win the fight in your heart?"

The grandfather answered. "The one I feed."

— anonymous, circulated on the internet

O then, what a blessed day will that be when I shall have all mercy, perfection of mercy, and fully enjoy the Lord of mercy; when I shall stand on the shore and look back on the raging seas I have sagely passed; when I shall review my pains and sorrows, my fears and tears, and possess the glory which was the end of all!

— Richard Baxter, *Weavings*, vol. 16, no. 2

Evil

O God of grace, give us your grace that we may not savor the evil in others in order to disguise the evil in ourselves. Amen.

— Jean Dalby Clift, *Women's Uncommon Prayers*, p. 255

An Epitaph

JOHN NEWTON, Clerk
Once an infidel and libertine
A servant of slaves in Africa,
Was, by the rich mercy of our Lord and Saviour
  JESUS CHRIST
Restored, pardoned, and appointed to preach
The Gospel which he had long laboured to destroy.
He ministered, near sixteen years in Olny, in Bucks,
And twenty-eight years in this Church.

— John Newton, the reformed slave ship commander and author of "Amazing Grace," authored his own epitaph, which is engraved in marble at the church of St. Mary Woolnoth, London

The radical (root) of the first word in the Chinese term for "repent" or "repentance" means "heart." The word for "heart" in its full presentation shows the four chambers. The concept of repentance is represented by two words, meaning "regret" and "correct," somewhat similar to the Greek concept of "metanoia."

Responding

Practicing Together:

- Give each person a newspaper from recent weeks. Invite them to scan the papers and clip any headlines, photos, or articles that raise a question of evil for them. Glue all the clippings on newsprint. Ask for comments from the group. Who or what is identified as evil in the collected clippings? How are we implicated? Who benefits from the evil, and how? What needs to be done to transform the evil? How might your community respond to the situation? What can children and youth do?

- Make a list of dark events in history. Discuss how the people of the day perceived the situation, and how, with hindsight, we perceive it today. Note the differences in viewpoint. Why is it sometimes easier to recognize evil with hindsight? Were these dark events undone, changed, or transformed at the time? If so, by whom, and how? What do we need to remember? Does anything about these events in the past still need undoing, changing, transforming today?

- Do you know people who have resisted evil or worked to transform it? Describe one person. What can you learn from their experiences and witness?

- Read Psalm 51 or another psalm of confession out loud. Have each person read one verse, slowly, pausing between each one. Try to imagine what may have caused the psalm writer to express the feelings in the psalm. Ask participants to take a few moments silently to remember a time when they felt similar feelings. Have the psalm read again by one person while the group members take a statue-like pose that expresses the feelings of the psalm. Read the collect for Ash Wednesday in the Prayer Book (p. 217). Find a musical settings of this psalm. Sing it together, or find and listen to a recording of it.

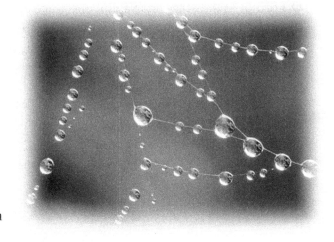

Practicing at Home:

- Pay attention to your dreams; they often will tell you about something "not right" in your life. Write the dreams in your journal. Don't think too much, or analyze as you write. Begin with some introductory phrase such as, "In this dream I saw/experienced ...," and then write quickly, allowing yourself to pour out anything and everything that comes to you. Over time, notice patterns, or consistent themes.

- Pay attention to your feelings of frustration or anxiety during the week—at work, when listening to a news broadcast, during a difficult conversation. Similarly, notice feelings of peace. What do you learn about your life from those feelings?

- In your journal, write about an instance in which you were the cause of a wrong. How did you make it right? If you have not yet made it right, how might you do so now in a way that will not cause further harm? What was/is the motivation behind your response?

- Place a simple, empty bowl in your home altar space. Imagine that it is a "begging bowl." At night, when you pray, hold the bowl and imagine that you are placing in it those things in your day which you regret. Offer them to God by holding the bowl up for a few moments.

— an activity learned from Bee Billups

Closing Prayer

Sing again the Opening Song, "De noche," which was sung in the time of Gathering.
Take a moment to share thanksgivings and personal prayer needs.
Close with the following prayers and blessing.

Grant, Lord God, to all who have been baptized into the death and resurrection of your Son Jesus Christ, that, as we have put away the old life of sin, so we may be renewed in the spirit of our mind, and live in righteousness and true holiness; through Jesus Christ our Lord, who lives and reigns with you, in the unity of the Holy Spirit, one God, now and for ever. Amen.

— "For All Baptized Christians," The Book of Common Prayer, p. 252

O Lord of Light: Rain your abundant grace upon us, that when the dark night of the soul threatens to overcome us, we may hear the comfort of your loving voice; in the name of the Father, and of the Son, and of the Holy Spirit, one God, Mother of us all. Amen.

— Elizabeth Rankin Geitz, Women's Uncommon Prayers, p. 313

May Almighty God, the Father of our Lord Jesus Christ, who has given us a new birth by water and the Holy Spirit, and bestowed upon us the forgiveness of sins, keep us in eternal life by his grace, in Christ Jesus our Lord. Amen.

— collect concluding the Renewal of Vows, Easter Vigil, The Book of Common Prayer, p. 294

August 7

This morning, just as I got in the kayak, a loon appeared at the bow of the boat! I grabbed the camera and think I caught it in silhouette, looking right at me! We have also lately been seeing two loons chasing each other across the water. They are amazingly fast. They flap their wings as if trying to take off to fly, then sort of run across the water. It is like a dance with quick, sharp twists and turns. I wonder if it is a territory issue? Or are they just playing?

Session Five

Will you proclaim by word and example the Good News of God in Christ?

Gathering

Place a small flask of oil near the bowl of water in the center of the group.

Around the bowl of water, place one votive candle (in a holder) for each person in the group.

OPENING SONG: **Go Tell It on the Mountain**

This Christmas spiritual can be expanded. Invite someone you know, perhaps a group member who writes poetry, to add verses that tell other parts of the Gospel story.

The refrain can be sung by all, the verses by an individual person.

While shepherds kept their watching
       o'er silent flocks by night,
    behold, throughout the heavens
       there shone a holy light.

The shepherds feared and trembled
       when lo! above the earth
    rang out the angel chorus
       that hailed our Savior's birth.

Down in a lowly manger
       the humble Christ was born,
    and God sent us salvation
       that blessed Christmas morn.

Refrain:
Go tell it on the mountain,
       over the hills and everywhere;
go tell it on the mountain,
       that Jesus Christ is born!
             — Afro-American spiritual,
              The Hymnal 1982, #99

ACTS 8:26–40   Philip and the Ethiopian Eunuch

Have this passage read as a dramatic dialogue. You will need a narrator, the angel/Spirit, Philip, and the eunuch.

Then the angel of the Lord said to Philip,

"Get up and go toward the south to the road that goes down from Jerusalem to Gaza."
(This is a wilderness road.) So he got up and went.

Now there was an Ethiopian eunuch, a court official of the Candace, queen of the Ethiopians,
in charge of her entire treasury. He had come to Jerusalem to worship and was returning home;
seated in his chariot, he was reading the prophet Isaiah.
Then the Spirit said to Philip,

"Go over to this chariot and join it."
So Philip ran up to it and heard him reading the
prophet Isaiah. He asked,

"Do you understand what you are reading?"
He replied,

"How can I, unless someone guides me?"
And he invited Philip to get in and sit beside him.

Now the passage of the scripture that he was reading
was this:

"Like a sheep he was led to the slaughter,
    and like a lamb silent before its shearer,
    so he does not open his mouth.
In his humiliation justice was denied him.
    Who can describe his generation?
For his life is taken away from the earth."

The eunuch asked Philip,

"About whom, may I ask you, does the prophet
say this,
    about himself or about someone else?"
Then Philip began to speak, and starting with
this scripture,
he proclaimed to him the good news about Jesus.

As they were going along the road, they came to some
water; and the eunuch said,

"Look, here is water! What is to prevent me from
    being baptized?"

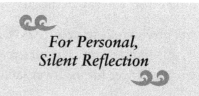

For Personal, Silent Reflection

Imagine it was you that the Spirit urged to witness to the eunuch. You hesitate to go to this foreigner, this unnamed man. Because he is a eunuch, he is excluded from becoming a fully righteous Jew. He is not someone with whom you would normally associate. Nevertheless you cautiously approach him, and are surprised to find out that he is reflecting on scripture and has questions. He invites you to come and sit with him in his chariot.

Spend a few moments wondering about the following:

Why is the eunuch willing, even eager, to talk with you?

How do you answer him?

How do you help him find his connection with Jesus?

He suddenly wants to be baptized. Why?

What do you do and say? Why do you do and say these things?

What might prevent you from baptizing him?

He commanded the chariot to stop, and both of them, Philip and the eunuch, went down into the water, and Philip baptized him. When they came up out of the water, the Spirit of the Lord snatched Philip away; the eunuch saw him no more, and went on his way rejoicing. But Philip found himself at Azotus, and as he was passing through the region, he proclaimed the good news to all the towns until he came to Caesarea.

Isaiah 12

A leader reads the two lines as marked below.

Assign a different small group of people to read each of the other sections.

As an alternative, you can sing this passage using the hymn settings in The Hymnal 1982, *#678 or #679.*

Leader: You will say in that day:

I will give thanks to you, O LORD,
> for though you were angry with me,
> your anger turned away, and you comforted me.

Surely God is my salvation;
> I will trust, and will not be afraid,
for the LORD GOD is my strength and my might;
> he has become my salvation.

Leader: With joy you will draw water from the wells
> of salvation. And you will say in that day:

Give thanks to the LORD,
> call upon his name;
make known his deeds among the nations;
> proclaim that his name is exalted.

Sing praises to the LORD, for he has done gloriously;
> let this be known in all the earth.
Shout aloud and sing for joy, O royal Zion,
> for great in your midst is the Holy One of Israel.

The Lord's Prayer

*A leader speaks or sings each line, and the group responds,
"Hallowed be thy name."*

*This can be sung to a West Indian folk melody.
See* The Presbyterian Hymnal, #589.

Our Father who art in heaven,
   —*Hallowed be thy name*—
Thy kingdom come, thy will be done,
   —*Hallowed be thy name*—
On earth as it is in heaven,
   —*Hallowed be thy name*—
Give us this day our daily bread,
   —*Hallowed be thy name*—
Forgive us all our trespasses,
   —*Hallowed be thy name*—
As we forgive those who trespass against us,
   —*Hallowed be thy name*—
And lead us not to the devil to be tempted,
   —*Hallowed be thy name*—
But deliver us from all that is evil,
   —*Hallowed be thy name*—
For thine is the kingdom, the power, and the glory,
   —*Hallowed be thy name*—
Forever and ever. Amen.
   —*Hallowed be thy name*—

Collect

Almighty God,
who gave to your apostles Philip and James
grace and strength to bear witness to the truth:
Grant that we, being mindful of their victory of faith,
may glorify in life and death the Name of our Lord Jesus Christ;
who lives and reigns with you and the Holy Spirit,
one God, now and forever. Amen.

> — collect for the feast of Saint Philip and Saint James,
> The Book of Common Prayer, p. 240

Sharing

FRESH OUT OF COLLEGE, I needed a job. Serendipitously, I was invited to live temporarily with an English family in Atlanta. There were seven children, six months to sixteen years of age. All but one of the children were boys. The infant, Robert, was born with a birth defect so severe that doctors were not certain how long he would live. He required constant care, which meant that the family needed the help of a nanny for a while.

That fall we met: A young Ohio country girl who went to church every Sunday, and a worldly British family who attended Theosophy meetings. We shared the care of Robert and took joy in each of his small developments. The day he first smiled and giggled was beyond belief. In the ensuing months, the parents and I sometimes had deep conversations. A few were about faith. Mostly we just shared life stories, including my family's experiences with Dad and his Parkinson's disease. The next spring, having found a second-grade teaching job, I set out on my own. Over the years, we continued to see each other. From time to time I would baby-sit for them. Robert grew and thrived in his own beautiful way. Although he could never care for himself, and never learned to talk, his simple love and joy in life was a gift to us all.

A few years later, one of the older brothers died suddenly and tragically. In the crisis of faith that ensued, the parents began to go to church. They said that something they saw in me, and in my family, led them there. We talked about God and prayer and faith. Robert was baptized. I was a sponsor for him. Eventually, with moves and life changes, we seldom saw each other, but we continued to stay in touch.

Robert lived to be twenty-three years old. They phoned when he died, and we talked a long while. Once again they spoke of their faith that pulled them through. Who could have guessed what God's grace would bring when our paths first crossed?

JOHNNY WAS A MEMBER of our parish. But that is not how we first came to know him. We first met Johnny when he came to the ecumenical soup kitchen that opened in our parish hall. Every weekday, a hot lunch was served. Johnny never missed it. Soon he started coming to church on Sunday. He always came early, and sat in the front row, right by the aisle. Then he started to bring some friends, Betty and Frank.

Johnny and his friends were developmentally disabled. It was hard to know how to respond to them. In our discomfort, none of us sat with them. That is until Liz, our matriarch and frequent social conscience, began to join him in his pew—the first one up front. Liz and Johnny befriended each other. Eventually Liz invited Johnny to join the church. He was eager. Liz saw to it that Johnny was confirmed.

One Sunday, late for the service, I plopped down next to Johnny and Liz (it was the easiest seat to reach from the side entrance). Everything went along predictably ... until the Eucharist. Johnny was the first one to reach the Communion rail that day; I followed him. As we knelt down, Johnny, looking even more radiant than usual, elbowed me. "Klara, I have something to tell you!"

With other things on my mind, I simply patted him on the arm and said, "That's great Johnny, now shhhh. You can tell me about it later." Johnny, however, could not contain his secret. With unbridled excitement, in front of God and everyone, he proclaimed—loud enough for the choir and the others kneeling at the altar to hear—"I'm so happy! I'm gonna get married!" He was full of joy and thanks for the gifts of God in his life. He simply *had* to tell someone. His eagerness shook my dutiful obedience and made me smile. I suspect that others smiled too.

It turned out that Johnny never did get married, but he and his

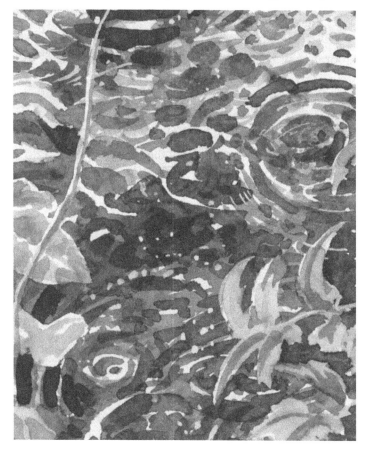

friends stayed with us. Liz and I continued to sit with him. Others began to do the same. As far as I know, he still attends the church and always sits in the front row (probably because he really does seem to enjoy being the first one up for Communion). Sometimes he served as crucifer or usher. We grew to love and listen to him. If he was absent, we worried about what was wrong. He attended my farewell party. A photo of him from that day sits on my desk. His glowing grin and sparkling eyes continue to greet me.

MY SMALL PARISH, Trinity Episcopal Church, is situated right next to the city park, located in the most diverse and economically challenged neighborhood in the state. In some pockets the poverty rate hovers at 70 percent. Over the last decade it has received over 8,000 immigrants, mostly of the Muslim faith, from Somalia, Burundi, Angola and other African countries.

The city is a recent recipient of a $30 million dollar "Choice Neighborhood" federal HUD grant, which will leverage another $100 million, for renewal of this neighborhood around Trinity. The grant proposal was created in partnership with "Healthy Neighborhoods," a grassroots collaborative of residents and organizations. Because of the intentional local input, the plan will transform the area, but will do so without displacing the people who already live there. It remarkably avoids the trap of gentrification.

About twenty-five years ago, when the mills collapsed and most other institutions abandoned the neighborhood, Trinity felt called to stay put and do all it could by, for and with those who lived nearby. Since then, the parish has been the parent of four public benefit organizations. By simply supporting the ideas of local people, first serving as fiscal sponsor and otherwise leveraging their institutional capacity, Trinity made things happen that would otherwise have been impossible.

Three of the resulting projects survive and are now independent non-profits that have become widely respected resources. They include Trinity Jubilee Center, a soup kitchen, food pantry and social service agency (begun thirty years ago, but still operating in the parish undercroft); Tree Street Youth, an after-school and summer program for youth; and the Center for Wisdom's Women, a weekday drop-in program for women for which I served as Executive Director for ten years. In 2019 the women's center opened a residential recovery community called Sophia's House, for women who have survived trafficking/exploitation and likely also incarceration and addiction.

Together these programs minister to hundreds of people every day through nonjudgmental, compassionate care, all free of charge.

Trinity's more recent efforts include the creation of a memorial garden in the church yard. It happened after Eddie, a soup kitchen guest, who also regularly attending Sunday worship, disappeared. Months later, his brother called saying Eddie had died and they needed a place to bury him. So we made a place and Eddie's ashes became the first of now a half dozen other local folks interred in the garden. Anyone who lives here, and does not have a church home or can't afford burial can be placed there. We offer a memorial service at no charge.

A few summers ago, after a murder in the park next door, a peace pole was added to the garden. Created by a local artist, it has "peace" written on it in a dozen languages that are now spoken by those who reside nearby. A neighborhood youth program called the Root Cellar made two wooden benches for the garden. We are now replanting the garden with only native plants that will feed beneficial local insects and birds, and invite pollinators. The project is becoming a witness to our care of the environment as we teach what is possible even in our urban area, and especially why it is needed. (Look for that story in the epilogue...) The garden is now an urban "pocket park," a safe and inviting respite in an area that has experienced violence and oppression.

The newest project coordinated by a Greg Boardman, parishioner who is a professional musician and locally loved music teacher, is a series of half hour mid-day concerts. His "Oasis of Music" provides and eclectic mix music each Wednesday in a relaxed, contemplative atmosphere. It also opens the beautiful and acoustically superb church to a wider audience. Two to three dozen folks regularly attend. Subtle evangelism at play.

The radical (root) in the word for "way" is a boat, signifying movement. As in English, "way" can be interpreted both as a physical path, and also as a methodology. What is curious in the Chinese context is that this same word is the "Tao" in Taoism, the Way, which predated the arrival of Christianity in China. Imagine Jesus' saying "I am the way, the truth, and the life" with this knowledge!

Our mission has been to be "A doorway to compassion and courage." Today, numbering only about a dozen folks, Trinity is on the cusp of discerning what our next call might be. We want our worship space to be open more than Sundays, and for the entire building to serve the neighborhood.

We have decided to deed the property to the Jubilee Center so that it can be renovated and expanded. It will create a bigger and better space for the Jubilee Center downstairs. The upstairs will become Trinity Commons, a public space or "third space"[1] for meetings, gatherings, performances, films, and other events. This letting go, will open our doors to even more people around us, those of all faiths, and it will assure the building continues our mission in and for our neighborhood, long into the future, whether or not we survive as a congregation or not.

The experiences and relationships in these ten square blocks, for over a decade, have affirmed for me the importance of taking the baptismal covenant seriously as a way of life. At Trinity we have especially learned about proclaiming the Good News by word and example, especially how to do so by example. A quote in my daily book of reflections recently summed it up: "In the end, it is not enough to think what we know. We must live it. For only by living it can Love show itself as the greatest principle" (Mark Nepo, *The Book of Awakening*, p. 140).

An East African Revelation

— by A. Theodore Eastman

DURING THE 1960S, when I served as Executive Secretary of The Overseas Mission Society, I made an extended field trip to East Africa. One of my priority destinations was the Diocese of Central Tanganyika in what is now Tanzania. I had come to know its bishop, an Australian named Alfred Stanway, through his visits to the United States, and I admired his missionary vision.

On my one Sunday in Central Tanganyika, I traveled with the bishop to a remote village where he was to do confirmations. Early that morning we boarded a light plane in the see city of Dodoma. The plane and pilot were provided by the Missionary Aviation Fellowship, a remarkable group that supplied transportation for missionaries of all kinds. After a bumpy ride, we landed on an equally bumpy grass field where we were greeted by several dozen village officials and local church leaders.

---

1 A third space is an "in-between or hybrid" or transitional communal space versus the duality of a home- and workspace, places where the individual can experience a transformative sense of self while being in relationship to others. https://www.brookings.edu/blog/up-front/2016/09/14/third-places-as-community-builders/

We had to walk some distance to the church which was nestled in a small valley. As we reached the brow of a hill above the valley, the church became visible. It was a simple structure with a roof and open sides. It appeared to seat two or three hundred. All around the church canvas tarpaulins had been rigged as extensions of the roof. The space under the tarps was jammed with people. When I remarked about this to Bishop Stanway, he explained that the confirmation class had completely filled the church, so that the rest of the congregation had to be accommodated under the canvas. He also pointed out that the confirmation class had been evangelized and prepared for baptism and confirmation, not by clergy, but by laity, some of whom had been trained and commissioned as catechists.

Bishop Stanway presided and preached in Swahili, which was translated for the people into Chigogo, the local tribal language, and for me into English, my tribal language. To expedite things the bishop laid hands on the candidates two-by-two. Halfway through the service, there was a tea break so that both bishop and people could refresh themselves. By the time we received the final blessing, more than four hours had elapsed.

Describe a time when someone asked you something about your faith.

> Was the person someone you knew already, or a stranger?

> Why did they ask a question about faith?

> Why did they chose you to answer their question?

> What did you respond?

> What was the result?

Recall occasions when you have proclaimed by example your experience of the Good News.

> When you proclaim by example, what happens to you?

> Is what you do everyday a witness to what you say you believe?

> Are your proclamations authentic?

> What is your motivation in sharing the Good News?

Think of someone who has proclaimed the Good News to you, in word or example. Name that person and briefly describe what happened.

> What was going on in your life at the time?

> What made it easier for you to hear what the person had to say?

> What things did this person do or say that spoke of his or her faith?

> What impact did these things have on you?

Reflecting

Scripture

Deuteronomy 6:4–9 The great commandment

1 Samuel 2:1–10   Hannah's song

Psalm 78:1–8   Teach the next generation

Matthew 3:1–17   John proclaiming in the desert
  (also Mark 1:2–8; Luke 3:1–17)

Matthew 5:13–16   Salt and light
  (also Mark 9:50; Luke 14:34–35)

Matthew 6:1–8   Warning against public piety

Matthew 23:1–7   Practice what you teach
  (also Mark 12:38–40; Luke 20:45–47)

Matthew 28:16–20   Commissioning of the disciples

Mark 6:6b–13   Disciples sent out in pairs
  (also Matthew 10:5–15; Luke 9:1–6)

Mark 7:31–37   Jesus cures the deaf man

Luke 1:46–55   Magnificat

Luke 4:14–21   Jesus goes to Galilee and teaches

Luke 5:1–11   Calling the first disciples
  (also Matthew 4:18-22; Mark 1:16–20)

Luke 6:46–49   The two foundations

Luke 8:4–8   Parable of the sower
  (also Matthew 13:1–9; Mark 4:1–9)

Luke 10:25–37   Good Samaritan

Luke 18:18–30   The rich young ruler
  (also Matthew 19:16–30; Mark 10:17–31)

Luke 19:1–10   Zaccheus

John 9   The man born blind receives sight

Romans 1:7–17   Paul gives thanks and shares the Gospel

James 2:14–26   Faith and works

1 John 1   Declaring God's message

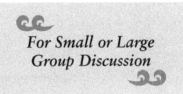

For Small or Large Group Discussion

Refer to the scripture selections. Choose one or two that speak to you, and discuss them.

What word or phrase jumps out at you?

What does the passage say to you?

What is it calling you to do?

Consider any of the suggested hymns that relate to your conversation. Read over the Prayer Book selections and comments.

What light do they shed on your conversation?

After a person is baptized, the priest places a hand on the person's head, and traces the sign of the cross (often with consecrated oil) on his/her forehead. Turn to page 308 in the Prayer Book, and read the words of consecration, and the subsequent words of welcome spoken by the congregation. The welcome is a reminder that the anointing comes with responsibility to act.

Take the flask of oil from beside the bowl of water, and pass it around the circle, inviting each person to put a dab of oil on a finger. Ask each person to turn and, with the oiled finger, trace the cross onto the forehead or hand of the next person. Do this while praying silently. Share your feelings about the experience.

If that mark of the cross were visible and permanent, would it change how you live?

Think about what it means, in the course of an average day, to act like a Christian.

How would someone know, just by watching you all day, that you are a Christian?

What do your checkbook and possessions say about your faith?

If it were illegal to be a Christian, would there be enough evidence to convict you?

Hymns

The Hymnal 1982
> Lord, you give the great commission, #528
> God is working his purpose out, #534
> O Zion, haste, #539

Lift Every Voice and Sing II
> I love to tell the story, #64
> I have decided to follow Jesus, #136
> Make me a blessing, #158
> This little light of mine, #160
> Go preach my gospel, #161
> Blessed assurance, #184

Wonder, Love, and Praise
> Will you come and follow me, #757
> We all are one in mission, #778
> Hallelujah! We sing your praises! #784

Book of Common Prayer

The Catechism, The Ministry, pp. 855–856
Postcommunion Prayer, p. 366
Prayers for the Church,
> "For the Mission of the Church," pp. 816, 257
Questions for parents and godparents at baptism,
> pp. 302–303
Welcome of the newly baptized, p. 308

My cousin Andrew is an on-fire new convert. He wants everyone to know it, and he wants everyone to have the exact same experience of conversion. He can't talk of anything without bringing God into the conversation. At least for now, his is a more conservative, black-and-white brand of Christianity than mine, and, sometimes, listening to him is tiring. We gently tell him enough is enough, and encourage him to find ways of proclaiming besides preaching. We remind him of St. Francis and of the phrase "See how they love each other!" Yet, it is a joy to watch this new charism in Andy, to see his life turn around, to be reminded of such passion and power.

The baptismal vow of proclamation is often equated with mission or evangelism, the sharing of the Good News with those who do not know it, in order to make more Christians and spread the church around the world. But this vow is not *the* mission vow (*all* the vows are about our mission). Neither is the vow about conversion. There is nothing here about being successful in bringing people into the fold. It only calls us to be faithful in proclaiming the Good News to believers and unbelievers alike, without concern for the consequences.

Joe Russell used to teach a training class for lay readers that was called "Proclaiming the Gospel as if You Believe It is Good News!" We have to proclaim as if we believe what we are saying is true. We also have to know exactly what it is we are proclaiming, because, in our biblically and spiritually illiterate culture, we cannot presume that people have somehow accidentally soaked up any knowledge of our faith. From these two suppositions—that we cannot proclaim what we do not believe and that we must know what we believe—a certain circular dynamism begins to generate: necessarily, to know the Good News inside out is to believe the Good News; and, necessarily, believing in the Good News compels us to proclaim it. We do not really have the option to be silent about our faith. Neither do we have the option to remain ignorant of it.

The Greek word *kerygma* ("good news" or "proclamation") traditionally has been used by the church to mean both the act of proclamation as well as that which is proclaimed. The very word itself is dynamic and integrative, an indication that the message and the medium are (or, let's say, *should be*) indistinguishable. Ultimately our very lives must become indistinguishable from the message and the medium. After all, the words we use when we proclaim the Good News will be authentic only if we strive to live what we proclaim. Actions speak louder than words—especially when our actions and our words are not as one.

We are invited into a way of being that is truly a "show-and-tell" of what we believe. When the living and the showing and the telling of our faith are totally integrated, our proclamation becomes powerful, even revolutionary. Consider the words of Mary in the Magnificat. Her words were confident, not meek and mild, and she put her life on the line. We are called to do no less.

You Walk Along Our Shoreline

You walk along our shoreline
where land meets unknown sea.
We hear your voice of power,
"Now come and follow me.
And if you still will follow
through the storm and wave and shoal,
then I will make you fishers,
but of the human soul."

You call us, Christ, to gather
the people of the earth.
We cannot fish for only
those lives we think have worth.
We spread your net of gospel
across the water's face,
our boat a common shelter
for all found by your grace.

We cast our net, O Jesus;
we seek your promised reign;
we work for love and justice;
we learn to hope through pain.
You call on us to gather
God's daughters and God's sons,
to let your judgment heal us
so that all may be one.

— Sylvia G. Dunstan,
The New Century Hymnal, #504

Gracious and Holy Father,
give us wisdom to perceive you,
diligence to seek you,
patience to wait for you,
eyes to behold you,
a heart to meditate on you
and a life to proclaim you,
through the power of the Spirit
of Jesus Christ our Lord. Amen.

— St. Benedict

Lord, you give the great commission:
    "Heal the sick and preach the word."
Lest the Church neglect its mission and
    the Gospel go unheard,
Help us witness to your purpose with
    renewed integrity;
With the Spirit's gifts empower us
    for the work or ministry.

Lord, you call us to your service:
    "In my name baptize and teach."
That the world my trust your promise,
    life abundant meant for each,
Give us all new fervor,
    draw us closer in community;
With the Spirit's gifts empower us
    for the work of ministry.

— *The Hymnal 1982,* #52, vs. 1 & 2,
Words: Jeffrey Rowthorn

Preach the Gospel at every opportunity, if necessary, use words.

— attributed to St. Francis

When it is darkest and it feels like it's all gone crazy, that is when…the light must shine. But it's salutary to remember Dr. King's wise admonition, that darkness cannot cast out darkness, only light can do that. Just as hatred cannot cast out hatred, only love, only love can do that… But now is not the time to hide this light under the bushel, now is the time to lift up this light, this light of the way of love is the light that we've gotten from Jesus, and let it shine even, and in spite of, whatever may happen around us. Now is the time when Thomas Cranmer's Advent collect rings true. "Almighty God, give us grace to cast away the works of darkness, and put on the armor of light." Now, now in the time of mortal life… please let this light shine.

— The Most Rev. Michael Curry, Presiding Bishop
(Executive Council 10/9/2020 sermon)

Discipleship is about focusing on Jesus, following in the footsteps of Jesus, becoming his hand and feet in the world. Discipleship is about loving as Jesus loves, giving as Jesus gives, forgiving as Jesus forgives, welcoming and including as Jesus welcomes and includes, doing justice and loving mercy and walking humbly with God, like Jesus. Matthew's gospel concludes with Jesus telling the disciples to "go therefore" and make disciples who make a difference in the world. "Go therefore" and be my hands, be my feet, be my face, be my voice, and change the world! (Matthew 28:19-20)

— The Most Rev. Michael Curry, Presiding Bishop
Crazy Christians: A Call to Follow Jesus

"You are the salt
of the earth…
You are the light
of the world…
Let your light so shine
that all who see you
will give glory
to your God."

— Jesus

God Speak to Me, That I May Speak

God speak to me, that I may speak
    in living echoes of your tone;
as you have sought, so let me seek
    your erring children lost and lone.

O lead me, God, that I may lead
    some wanderers along life's way;
O feed me so that I may feed
    your hungry ones without delay.

O fill me with your fullness, God,
    your overflowing love to know;
in glowing word and kindling thought,
    your love to tell, your praise to show.

O use me, God, use even me
    just as you will, and when, and where,
until your blessed face I see,
    your rest, your joy, your glory share.
— Frances Ridley Havergal

The concern of parents and religious educators is not to teach the faith but to help people feel themselves to be part of the faith story that shapes our understanding of God's creative action in our lives and the world about us ... if the story is not familiar, then the baptismal font remains but a strange furnishing in a world where water is available at the turn of a tap and God's mystery passes before our eyes unseen ...

— Joe Russell, *Sharing Our Biblical Story*, pp. 2–3

What is the ministry of the laity? ...to represent Christ and his church; to bear witness to him wherever they may be; and, according to the gifts given them, to carry on Christ's work of reconciliation in the world; and to take their place in the life, worship, and governance of the Church.

— The Book of Common Prayer, p. 855, Catechism

Make a friend,
Be a friend,
Bring a friend
to Christ.

— The Cursillo movement

And now, Father, send us out to do the work you have given us to do, to love and serve you as faithful witnesses of Christ our Lord. Amen.

— Postcommunion Prayer, The Book of Common Prayer, p. 366

And, we pray, give us such an awareness of your mercies,
that with truly thankful hearts we may show forth your praise,
not only with our lips, but in our lives,
by giving up ourselves to your service,
and by walking before you in holiness and righteousness all our days…

— The Book of Common Prayer, p. 101, The General Thanksgiving

"We must learn to tell the Gospel stories,
   do so as often as possible, and most importantly,
   always tell them as if we believe they really are
   GOOD NEWS!"

— Heard at a training for lay readers by Joe Russell

Benediction

Go forth into the world in peace;
be of good courage;
hold fast that which is good;
render to no one evil for evil;
strengthen the fainthearted;
support the weak;
help the afflicted;
honour everyone;
love and serve the Lord,
rejoicing in the power of the Holy Spirit;
and the blessing of God Almighty,
the Father, the Son, and the Holy Ghost,
be amongst you and remain with you always.
Amen.

— The Book of Common Prayer 1892, 1928

Celtic Prayer

The sacred Three be over me
with my working hands this day
with the people on my way
with the labor and the toil
with the land and with the soil
with the tools that I take
with the things that I make
with the thoughts of my mind
with the sharing with mankind
with the love of my heart
with each one that plays a part
the sacred Three be over me
the blessings of the Trinity.

— Found in *Ministry in Daily Life: A
   Guide to Living the Baptismal Covenant*,
   Episcopal Church Center, 1996

Responding

Practicing Together:

• Share stories of your favorite vacation experience. Notice the way in which you told of your experience (your gestures and feelings). Name your favorite Bible stories or passages. Form small groups (in pairs or, at most, groups of three) and tell a portion of the biblical story with the same enthusiasm as you shared a vacation story. One person takes the role of the proclaiming, the other person the role of someone who has not heard the Good News. Then trade roles. When everyone has finished, gather the whole group and sing the hymn "I love to tell the story," *Lift Every Voice and Sing II*, #64.

• Think of someone you know who has not heard the Good News. Think about how you might share your faith with them. Do you worry about coming across as obnoxious? What would make sharing easier for you? How might you share in a way that feels authentic to you, yet is attuned to whether your audience is receptive? When was the last time you shared the Good News of God? Was it by word or example? How did it go? Have you prayed for that person?

• Consider starting a "Guild of Biblical Storytellers" in your church. The members would be available to proclaim a part of the story at any time the community is gathered. Consult the book, *Story Journey*, by Thomas E. Boomershine. Another good resource is the Network of Biblical Storytellers website (www.nbsint.org).

• The last five psalms in the Bible all express adoration and praise of God. Choose one of them and have it read by someone who can do so in a dramatic way, in a loud voice. Ask each person to speak one word (just one) that jumps out at them. List the words of praise and adoration in the psalm and then add other words that come to mind. As a group, read the list out loud, repeatedly and with enthusiasm.

• Take a look at your church and its activities. What is proclaimed explicitly and implicitly by your building, your worship style, your behavior, outreach activities, the budget? Are these the ways in which you would like people to know you? Do you need to change anything that does not represent how you want to be known?

• What sort of person is missing from your church community? To whom might you reach out? What do you need to do in order to become an inviting community? Think of a place in which you do not feel welcome. What made you feel that way?

- Give everyone an old magazine. Ask them to clip out bunches of advertisements, and make a collage by pasting them onto large pieces of newsprint. Post the collages in the meeting space. What is proclaimed there? Note any that demand a response from your community. What might be a next step?

- If you have a college campus near you, reach out to the students. Talk with the college chaplain about campus ministry and how you might fill gaps in the campus program. Particularly try to build relationships with exchange students.

- Have a "Hymn Sing" in your church, one that focuses on older Gospel hymns. Or buy a good recording of Gospel music and listen to it. Sing, clap, or even dance as you listen. What do you feel and learn?

Practicing at Home:

- Think of someone you know who have not heard the Good News. Think about how you might share your faith with them. Do you worry about coming across as obnoxious? What would make sharing easier for you? How might you share in a way that feels authentic to you, yet is attuned to your audience? When was the last time you shared the Good News of God? Was it by word or example? How did it go? Have you prayed for that person?

- When you are first getting to know someone, what are some of the important things that you like to share about yourself? Think of something that is important to you to tell people. How do those conversations arise? What makes it comfortable for you to share? What signals you that the person wants to hear more? That they have heard enough? How do you close such a conversation in a way that allows it to open again later?

- Write a short letter as an "Epistle," pretending you are addressing a group of new Christians. Make your first paragraph one that proclaims the Good News.

- Most stories in the Gospels originated from an oral tradition of storytelling. The stories were told, person to person and generation to generation, before they were ever written down. If all the Bibles disappeared tomorrow, could you reconstruct the story? Learn one Gospel story by heart and tell it to someone else. What do you suppose led you to pick that story? How does it connect with your life?

- The quote *"Preach the Gospel at every opportunity. If necessary, use words."* is often attributed to St. Francis of Assisi. While in keeping with his life, there is no record of him ever saying it, and in his life, he is quite known for his preaching in words, especially to the rich. There is, however, record of him saying something similar: *"It is no use walking anywhere to preach unless our walking is our preaching."* Think about and discuss the relationship between proclaiming by word and example. Share stories of when you proclaimed either by word or example. Which do you do more? Try to do more of the other. (https://www.huffpost.com/entry/preach-the-gospel-at-all-times-st-francis_b_1627781.)

Closing Prayer

Sing again the Opening Song, "Go tell it on the mountain," which was sung in the time of Gathering.
Take a moment to share thanksgivings and personal prayer needs.
Close with the following prayer and blessing.

Risen Savior, you first appeared to Mary Magdalene, the apostle to the apostles: Help us hear you when you call our names, that we, too, may proclaim the good news of your resurrection throughout the world, to the honor and glory of your name. Amen.

— Elizabeth Rankin Geitz, *Women's Uncommon Prayers*, p. 316

May the Spirit of truth lead us into all truth, give us grace to confess that Jesus Christ is Lord, and to proclaim the wonderful works of God; and the blessings of God Almighty, the Father, the Son, and the Holy Spirit, be among us, and remain with us always. Amen.

— Seasonal Blessings, Advent, *The Book of Occasional Services* (adapted)

Invite everyone to take one of the votive candles and light it.
Sing the song, "This little light of mine," found in Lift Every Voice and Sing, *#221.*
Invite each person to take a candle home.

August 10

Today the chick was all alone when I first got to my hidden spot.
And it was diving! Every now and then it let out a plaintive little
cry. The parents were not far off. They answered and soon
appeared. The first steps of independence. Such a small thing all
alone! It made our little lake feel rather big. It worries me that
someone has set up some sort of water-skiing course right there in
the area where the loons seem to be raising the chick.

Session Six

Will you seek and serve Christ in all persons,
loving your neighbor as yourself?

Gathering

Lay a couple of hand towels beside the bowl of water.
In large, easily legible letters, print the "Hand-washing Prayer" from the Reflecting section.
Place the prayer next to the towels.

OPENING SONG   Ubi caritas

There is a Taizé setting of this hymn in Wonder, Love, and Praise, *#831*
Four adaptations with verses are in The Hymnal 1982, *#576, #577, #581, and #606*
Translation: Where true charity and love abide, God is there.

Ubi caritas
    et amor,
Ubi caritas,
    Deus ibi est.

        — Latin, 8th century

JOHN 13:1–17   Jesus Washes the Disciples' Feet

Have three group members read the parts of the narrator, Peter, and Jesus.

Now before the festival of the Passover, Jesus knew that his hour had come to depart from this world and go to the Father. Having loved his own who were in the world, he loved them to the end. The devil had already put it into the heart of Judas son of Simon Iscariot to betray him. And during supper Jesus, knowing that the Father had given all things into his hands, and that he had come from God and was going to God, got up from the table, took off his outer robe, and tied a towel around himself. Then he poured water into a basin and began to wash the disciples' feet and to wipe them with the towel that was tied around him. He came to Simon Peter, who said to him,

    "Lord, are you going to wash my feet?"

Jesus answered,
> "You do not know now what I am doing,
> > but later you will understand."

Peter said to him,
> "You will never wash my feet."

Jesus answered,
> "Unless I wash you, you have no share with me."

Simon Peter said to him,
> "Lord, not my feet only
> > but also my hands and my head!"

Jesus said to him,
> "One who has bathed does not need to wash,
> > except for the feet,
> > > but is entirely clean.
> And you are clean, though not all of you."

For he knew who was to betray him;
> for this reason he said,
> "Not all of you are clean."

After he had washed their feet, had put on his robe,
and had returned to the table, he said to them,
> "Do you know what I have done to you?
> You call me Teacher and Lord—
> > and you are right, for that is what I am.
> So if I, your Lord and Teacher, have washed
> > your feet, you also ought to wash
> > one another's feet.
> For I have set you an example, that you also
> > should do as I have done to you.
> Very truly, I tell you, servants are not greater
> > than their master, nor are messengers
> > greater than the one who sent them.
> If you know these things, you are blessed if you do
> them."

For Personal, Silent Reflection

There is no record of the Last Supper in the Gospel of John. Instead we find the story of Jesus washing the feet of his disciples. Washing the feet of others is something that was done only by servants. Jesus has taken off his robe and tied a towel around his waist. He takes a bowl and a pitcher of water and kneels to wash the feet of his disciples. When he approaches Peter, Peter resists the gesture. Spend a few moments in silence and imagine what Peter is feeling.

Why does he resist so mightily?

Why does he change his mind?

If you had been there, how would you have responded to Jesus?

What would you have said?

Isaiah 41:17–20

Have each of the first six phrases below
(as indicated by line spaces) read by a different person.

The final phrase (as marked) is read by all.

When the poor and needy seek water,
  and there is none,
  and their tongue is parched with thirst,

I the LORD will answer them,
  I the God of Israel will not forsake them.

I will open rivers on the bare heights,
  and fountains in the midst of the valleys;

I will make the wilderness a pool of water,
  and dry land springs of water.

I will put in the wilderness the cedar,
  the acacia, the myrtle, and the olive;

I will set in the desert the cypress,
  the plane and the pine together,

All: So that all may see and know,
  all may consider and understand,
  that the hand of the LORD has done this,
  the Holy One of Israel has created it.

The Lord's Prayer in Spanish

Padre nuestro que estás en el cielo,
  santificado sea tu Nombre,
  Venga tu reino,
  hágase tu voluntad,
  en la tierra como en el cielo.
Danos hoy nuestro pan de cada día.
Perdona nuestras ofensas,
  como también nosotros perdonamos
  a los que nos ofenden.
No nos dejes caer en tentación
  y líbranos del mal.
Porque tuyo es el reino,
  tuyo es el poder,
  y tuya es la gloria,
  ahora y por siempre. Amén.

— La Santa Eucaristía: Rito Dos,
El Libro de Oración Común

Collect

Heavenly Father, whose blessed Son
came not to be served but to serve:
Bless all who, following in his steps,
give themselves to the service of others;
that with wisdom, patience, and courage,
they may minister in his Name
to the suffering, the friendless, and the needy;
for the love of him who laid down his life for us,
your Son our Savior Jesus Christ,
who lives and reigns with you and the Holy Spirit,
one God, for ever and ever. Amen.

— "For Social Service," The Book of Common Prayer, p. 260

Sharing

IN MY SECOND YEAR as a teacher, I had the first-grade class. Andrew was one of my students. Academically, he was an average child, I think, although I don't really remember. What I do remember is that he was small, awkward, and gangly; that his hair was thin and mousy; that his nose always seemed to be runny; and that his large, thick glasses insisted on resting halfway down his always runny nose. Whenever Andrew wanted to talk with me—which was often—he invaded my space by standing as close as possible. He was an ugly duckling, and we all tried to avoid him—children and teachers alike.

And then one day, as always happens with ugly ducklings, there came this sudden, remarkable change. But this is an ugly duckling story with one difference: Andrew didn't change himself, as ugly ducklings usually do—Andrew changed me.

One day, because some program was being held in the school's lunchroom, we had to eat our noon meal in the classroom. Just as I had finished lining up the children with their dimes in hand to go buy milk, Andrew came up and attached himself to me by tugging at my sleeve. In his stuffy, nasal voice he said that he could not find his lunchbox. I shooed him away, saying he needed to look harder. We waited for him while he looked some more. A few moments later, he was back, observing that, not only was his lunchbox lost, but that his milk money was in the lost lunchbox. We could wait no longer. "OK, Andrew!" I sighed impatiently, and, planting a dime in his hand, I told him to go get some milk. Turning to the class I asked who might

share some lunch with Andrew. A couple of children readily agreed, and off we went to buy our milk.

Halfway through lunch, another child, Jimmy, timidly came up to me to say that he had found Andrew's lunchbox—in the bottom of the construction paper scrap box. I called for Andrew and had Jimmy return the lunch box. Andrew's response was a surprising one. Even though it was obvious that someone had hidden his lunchbox just to pick on him, Andrew joyously whipped the box open and extracted the dime inside. Then he exclaimed, "Oh, I am so happy you found my box, because now I can give 'Miss T' back the dime she gave me for milk!" He beamed at me with his toothless grin and a sparkle in his eyes, as he held up the dime for me to take.

In a flash, I felt Andrew's heart of gold. It was a heart that had the power to transform mine. He was not angry or hurt at having been teased. He was not spiteful or bitter in return. He simply loved.

> Let the little children come to me ... for it is to such as these that the kingdom of heaven belongs.

I left the room to regain my composure. Upon returning, I began to be a different teacher, and Andrew became one of my favorite kids. Andrew was still a scrawny and clingy child, but my vision had changed, and he was now a swan in my eyes. From that day forward, I watched and listened to him. His presence daily taught me about love.

John
— by Van Gardner

THE DON MILLER HOUSE, in Baltimore, Maryland, is a Hospice ministry for people with AIDS. It is a remarkable place of gentleness and caring begun some years ago by an interfaith group determined to meet the AIDS crisis with love and compassion, rather than the judgment that had marked so much of the religious response in those fearful early days. John was a resident of the Don Miller House. Dorris, a member of our congregation who works at the house and lives her baptismal covenant as if it were in her genes, brought him to church.

At first, John stayed at the edge of our community, worshiping at the Thursday evening Taizé "Service for Peace and Reconciliation." Then, he occasionally began to attend the Sunday morning Eucharist. He was very quiet and seemed frail. The disease was, by now, quite far advanced. In time, we began to prepare, together, for his death. We met in his room at the house, which was full to overflowing with memorabilia, photos, candles, and religious images and icons that suggested a deep yearning to connect with something beyond, something eternal.

John's life, like his room, was cluttered. Growing up in rural West Virginia and knowing himself to be gay from a young age, he had met with only rejection from family, neighbors, community, and church. Among his litany of regrets was a daughter whom he had not seen since she was very young and who still lived in West Virginia. He hoped to see her again.

As priest, I found I had little to offer John, and little to say, in front of all the broken pieces of his life. I could only provide a prayerful, listening presence, and the love of an accepting community of faith.

One morning, after the Sunday Eucharist, I noticed John waiting quietly as I greeted some of the folks who are part of our open and generous community. When the last person had passed out the door, John approached me with a simple request: "Can I be baptized?" He had been receiving communion, and I had assumed he was baptized. It never occurred to me to ask. "Of course," I said. Soon, we were back in his cluttered rooms making plans, not for his funeral, but for his baptism.

In time I asked the obvious question: "Why do you want to be baptized?" I was sure I knew the answer: something to do with preparing for his death and putting things right with God. And maybe I was partially correct, but what he said surprised me. "I've been in lots of churches in my life, but this is the first place I've been that accepted me as I am."

On a bright Sunday morning we gathered in the church, and, with John's permission, I shared something of his story. John then stood at the font (which sits centrally and prominently at the crossing of the cathedral church) and was washed with the water of baptism. Together the congregation sang, "Alleluia, Alleluia, Alleluia," and welcomed John into the household of faith. It was an occasion during which we were not simply attending church; we *became* church—the body of Christ embracing one of God's own.

In the weeks that followed, Dorris and others at the Don Miller House arranged for John's daughter to come for a visit. At the end of his life, John came to know something of the abundant grace of God. When he died, his funeral was held at the cathedral, and, as the congregation gathered at the table for Holy Eucharist, each person passed the font and touched the water that holds the promise.

I've often said that "baptism is a sacrament of community." With John, the words took on new meaning. God had always loved and cherished John. Now, through a community of people who accepted and welcomed him, John, finally, came to know God's love and grace. And we—who knew something of God's love and grace already—received it, thanks to John, even more abundantly.

Good News: God Delivers

— by Kathy Bozzuti-Jones

I AWAKENED THIS MORNING recalling a sweet encounter from the night before. The memory stayed with me because it was poignant—but also because, in my mindfulness training, I have been practicing present-moment awareness, and so I am more able to remember how things went down and even, sometimes, how they fit together.

A series of simple choices last night began with a moment of irritation followed by a moment of self-indulgence, which turned into the unlikely (and holy) welcome of a holy stranger. *Sometimes, a simple act of kindness can remind you who you are and, perhaps, even more so, who you want to become.*

As I sat on the bed, annoyed that our son had missed dinner without a word of notice, I had the urge to boycott the family movie night he had proposed earlier. I noted my annoyance, then my urge to boycott, then my self-criticism for not being more forgiving, then my realization that I was simply stuck. Typically, these feelings would lump into one big uncomfortable feeling but, as I said, I've been practicing noticing the stream of movements and reactions within, so I can remember the details of what happened next.

My story begins in the next moment. The first move—was it self-indulgence or was it loving care? I picked up the phone and ordered delivery of three overpriced pints of guilt-free ice cream, in our three favorite flavors. More typical of me, I would wait for it to go on sale and then wait three more days for it to be delivered. My father's depression-era ethic, I guess. His immigrant father would wait for the sale, walk to the store, and then carry home enough to last for weeks, but that's another story. I was hoping to lift my mood and surprise my family.

Not five minutes after I placed the order, my son entered with an apology that melted my cold heart (a bit). And five minutes after that the phone rang, and a man with a heavy accent offered another apology because they were out of one of the ice cream flavors. He went on to list all the alternatives, but I couldn't quite make out any of the words except for "strawberry," so I ordered that one. Behind the accent was a conciliatory voice and so I let it go. Then I calculated the twenty minutes it would take for the delivery to arrive and looked forward to our night together.

About forty minutes later, in the middle of our movie, my phone rang again. The same voice said that he had gotten all the way to our apartment but had forgotten to put the delivery in his car, so had to turn back. Again, he seemed so gentle in his apology, I just asked him to calculate how long it would take to return. Thirty minutes, he said. Knowing how unlikely that prospect was, I thanked him, and he thanked me for my patience.

About forty-five minutes later, my phone rang again. I recognized the voice and made out that he was here. I thanked him and he asked me to come down to receive the delivery. This not being pandemic protocol and, having already tipped him for his service, I suggested he just leave the package in the lobby. But he persisted.

At this point, I got a funny feeling. I couldn't quite put my finger on it, but the tone of his voice had changed. So I asked my husband if he would go to greet the man downstairs.

A short time later, he returned with a single pint of ice cream! And it was shrunken inside, partly melted and with a coating of freezer burn! But my husband had a noticeably calm and gentle look on his face from the moment he lifted the foil-covered pint out of the bag. I'm sorry, he said. This is what we have. The world's most expensive pint of ice cream, I thought. Did you get a refund? Well, no. He then went on to tell me about his encounter with the delivery man.

He was so sorry. He had forgotten the other two pints. He was so sorry; if we were to call his employer to complain, he said, he would certainly lose his job. I thought about all the people out of work since the pandemic began. I thought about all the immigrants being targeted and humiliated in our country. Perhaps Mark thought about that too. More likely, in that moment, he saw the desperation in the man's eyes as he reached into his pocket for whatever he had and explained that he couldn't come close to refunding the balance.

Normally, I'd be pretty annoyed—mostly with myself for overpaying in the first place. But I wasn't annoyed at all. And I didn't mind a bit forgoing dessert altogether. There was something about the man's voice, Mark's facial expression, and the mental image of this conversation happening before the lobby attendant. What are the chances that this man's double slip-up would happen on an order from a priest and a minister? He would never know that we weren't just randomly compassionate, but,

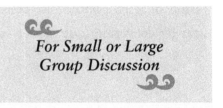

For Small or Large Group Discussion

Recall a time when you were surprised by someone's showing Christ's love to you.

How did you feel?

Recall a recent time when you showed Christ's love to someone close to you; to someone who was a stranger.

What made you do it?

Think of someone that you have found to be very hard to love.

What caused your hard feelings?

What is it about your relationship with that person that makes it difficult?

How might the relationship be transformed?

Recall a time when you avoided an opportunity to share Christ's love with someone.

Why did you not do so?

rather, practicing (licensed even!) compassion-bearers. And the look of relief on his face, both witnessed and imagined, was its own reward.

An hour later, as I readied for bed, the phone beeped a text notification. It had a series of "thanks" and praying hands emojis in a repeating pattern. It made me smile. I showed Mark and asked whether he wanted me to comment. He said, "Yes, tell him I told you that he is a good man, a sign from God, and offer him our blessings."

Just as I was drifting off to sleep came the reply: Thanks. [Praying hands emoji.] "Big hard [heart] you and [you're] husband. Thanks thanks thanks. [Praying hands emoji.] I really happy. Thanks. Thanks."

God is good. And there is hope, I thought, in the small encounters that humanize us and dignify one another. Hate and xenophobia, like death, will not have the last word. There was an empty carton of freezer-burned ice cream on the counter to remind me not to be afraid. And a holy stranger delivering good news to remind me of who I want to be.

Sophie

MY LITTLE DOG, a thirteen-pound miniature poodle named Sophie, is a rescue from a puppy mill. That means she spent the first six years of her life in a crate, in a barn with piles of other crated dogs, bred every six months. Human contact was minimal, and likely only harsh. She was not groomed, walked, or held. She was fed lousy food and left to pee in the crate.

When Sophie came to me from Missouri, she would not look anyone in the eye, her docked tail was usually tucked between her legs and never wagged. She kept her distance, and if you touched her, she flinched. To this day any sharp noise makes her run. The vet says it is because in the puppy mill, when dogs are barking, they run down the rows of crates banging a metal bar against the metal crates to get the dogs to shut up. Sophie does not know how to play with humans or other dogs. I had to teach her how to go up and down stairs. She will not take any food from your hand, even the best tidbit or meat, or her favorite treat (a carrot). It has to be put on the floor. Then she grabs it and runs off before eating it.

Slowly a gentle spirit began to emerge. After she was with me for a few months, one day, sitting at my desk, I felt something on my leg. When I looked down, it was Sophie, poking my leg with her nose. It was her first piece of communication. That sweet behavior has continued, though sometimes now an annoying habit, that becomes more and more rapid and forceful if ignored, accompanied by a whine. Since then, she has learned to prance and play bow after doing her business, or when it is chow time.

For seven years, Sophie has been safe, deeply loved and cared for. Yet any sharp noise and she still scurries off. "What was that?!" I always exclaim, "Oh, it's OK!" Now she can shake it off and quickly return. When anyone nearby is anxious, angry, or high energy, she begins to tremble and wants to be picked up. She will now look at me in the eye, but never strangers. Every night before bed, I have massaged her entire body. She can now be petted without flinching, as long as she sees your hand coming. If touched from behind, she still jumps.

Sophie's behaviors today are echoes of her first six years of isolation and abuse. I see the same responses in people I know who have struggled with early childhood trauma, who have been trafficked or otherwise exploited, have been incarcerated, or have struggled with addiction and mental illness—no eye contact, easily startled at noises or when touched, trembling when triggered. Other learned behaviors for coping and safety might be being angry, confrontational, or even violent, a response often seen in other abused dogs, though not Sophie.

We "rescue" dogs by the thousands. When treated humanely they begin to heal from their trauma, though like Sophie, because of the scars, she may never be a "normal" dog. I have often wondered why, if we can understand this about dogs, we can't understand it about human beings?

What might happen if we simply strive to be present, listen, and hold the stories of those wounded by life, until bit by bit, trust grows enough for bodies, minds, and souls to begin to heal? Of course, the safe containers of shelter, food, and treatment are also needed. But it seems to me the missing pieces are listening and loving.

When will we start asking "What happened to you?!" instead of confronting those who have been wounded in life with the question "What is wrong with you?" Wouldn't that be better than isolating people in prisons or leaving them alone to fend for themselves on the street?

Reflecting

Scripture

Genesis 18:1–8   The Lord visits Abraham

Leviticus 19:17–18 Love, not hate

Matthew 5:1–12   Beatitudes
(also Luke 6:20–23)

Matthew 5:14–16   Let your light so shine

Matthew 10:40–42   Who welcomes you, welcomes me
(also Mark 9:41)

Matthew 22:34–40   The Greatest Commandment
(also Mark 12:28–34; Luke 10:25–28)

Matthew 25:31–40   When I was thirsty

Mark 9:33–37   Whoever wants to be first must be last
(also Matthew 18:1–5; Luke 9:46–48)

Mark 12:41–44   The widow who gave all she had
(also Luke 21:1–4)

Luke 6:27–36   Love your enemies
(also Matthew 5:38–48)

Luke 7:36–50   Woman who washes Jesus' feet with her tears

Luke 10:25–37   Parable of the Good Samaritan

John 15:1–18   Jesus, the true vine; love one another

Romans 13:8–10   Love sums up all law, all commandments

1 Corinthians 13   The gift of love

Hymns

The Hymnal 1982

    Lord, you give the great commission, #528
    O Zion, haste, thy mission high fulfilling, #539
    Remember your servants, Lord, #560
    Morning glory, starlit sky, #585
    Lord, whose love through humble service, #610
    O Master, let me walk with thee, #660

Wonder, Love, and Praise

    You laid aside your rightful reputation, #734
    We all are one in mission, #778
    Hallelujah! We sing your praises! #784

The New Century Hymnal

    Won't you let me be your servant? #539
    Jesu, Jesu, #498

The Book of Common Prayer

    The Catechism: The New Covenant, pp. 850–851
    Postcommunion Prayers, pp. 339, 365
    A Form of Commitment to Christian Service, pp. 420–421
    "For the Poor and Neglected," p. 826

The word for "love" is an ideogram, composed of three elements: receive, heart, and friend. Therefore, to love is also to make oneself open and vulnerable to be loved by the other.

For Small or Large Group Discussion

Refer to the scripture selections. Choose one or two that speak to you and discuss them.

What word or phrase jumps out at you?

What does the passage say to you?

What is it calling you to do?

Consider any of the suggested hymns that relate to your conversation. Read over the prayer book selections and comments.

What light do they shed on your conversation?

At one point in my spiritual journey, burned out on church, I spent a whole year worshiping with the Society of Friends, the Quakers. The meeting I regularly attended was a "silent" one, meaning there was no planned program. We gathered for an hour each Sunday, and prayerfully sat together in silence. Occasionally someone spoke a few words in the silence, a shared thought that was given them by the Spirit. Over the course of the year, they taught me much, and I felt very much a part of them. I joined in their monthly potluck lunches, and even participated in their annual Easter weekend retreat. I was constantly struck by the community's hospitality, not only to me, but to strangers. At one point in the year, a "traveling friend" appeared. The person was welcomed and housed for the duration of her stay, and in exchange brought the wishes and news of other meetings she had visited.

At meetings, the community members used the archaic pronouns "thee" and "thou." These words once represented informal forms of the singular, second-person pronoun ("you," when used singularly, being the formal form). "Thee" and "thou" were used to address children, intimates, servants, and, interestingly, God. The societal rules that went along with the grammatical rules for these pronouns were complicated: sometimes "thee" and "thou" established intimacy, when used with friends, and sometimes established hierarchy, when used with servants; sometimes they were reserved for domestic use and other times for public use, as in common prayer. Anyone who has studied a modern language that retains informal/formal grammatical forms knows how hard it is. When I was studying Hungarian in Hungary I often, embarrassingly, got it all wrong, and was forever accidentally insulting shopkeepers or elders!

While Quakers today may not use these pronouns exactly as did the drafters of the King James Bible (for example, I have heard Quakers use "thee" and "thou" interchangeably), they do seem to understand the richness of paradox involved. "Thee" and "thou" sound more, not less, formal to modern ears, and therefore facilitate worship by sounding appropriately auspicious and reverent. More importantly, Quakers take full theological advantage of the fact that the only broad usage of "thee" and "thou" remaining in modern English is in direct address to God; therefore, when they turn these pronouns back upon each other, they consciously are making a very powerful statement. As it was explained to me, this usage expresses the concept held by the Society of Friends that the Light of God is in everyone. Our job is to see it and honor it. To help my understanding, they gave me Thomas Kelly's little book *Testament of Devotion* to read. I have since connected the attitudes espoused in Kelly's book to those of other faiths and disciplines. Those who practice Hinduism, bowing with hands at the chest and palms together, greet the holy in each with the word "namaste."

Such an attitude has an application in everything we think and do—the difference, for example, between approaching someone with open palms facing outward and upward in a gesture of receiving, instead of hands clenched or facing downward. This attitude, as expressed by Jesus when he said, "I no longer call you servants; I call you friends," calls us into closer, yet ever more respectful—even reverent—relationship to one another. Maria Harris practices this kind of intimate respect in her teaching. When asked what she teaches, she does not answer with the subject matter ("I teach theology"); instead, she responds: "I teach students." Her point is that each student is the subject, not the object, of her teaching. She strives to be present to the learners as people. The content to be mastered becomes the object they share.

The vow—to seek and serve Christ in everyone—guides us in proclaiming the Good News in our actions, at a very personal level. I remember once being with a friend, Donald, in New York. He had recently moved from Maine to take a job in the "Big Apple." I was concerned about how he would get along in the city. My worry was for naught. One morning, I accompanied him into the city as he went to work. I noticed that he bought two coffees in the commuter rail station near his suburban home. I didn't think that much about the extra coffee until we boarded the train and Donald handed it to the conductor (something, I came to learn, that he did regularly). Upon arriving in the city, before we left Grand Central Terminal, he paused to purchase a bunch of flowers. A block later, he stopped to greet a young woman who lived on the street; her home was a small nook in a building. He greeted her by name, exclaimed "Happy Birthday," and gave her the flowers. She beamed, and then cried. So did Donald. They talked a bit, shared God's blessing, and we moved on.

On my next visit to New York, I again accompanied Don into the city. As we returned home on the train that night, the loudspeaker came on just before Don's stop. It was the conductor singing "Happy Birthday" to Don.

For Small or Large Group Discussion

Take some time to recall the foot-washing liturgies you have attended.
If you never have witnessed this liturgy, you may want to familiarize yourself with it by reading the "Maundy Thursday" section in the Prayer Book (pp. 274–275) and the section called "On Maundy Thursday" in *The Book of Occasional Services*.

How did you participate? As an observer? By having your feet washed? If so, who washed them?

Or did you wash the feet of others? If so, whose feet did you wash?

How did these activities make you feel?

In pairs, go to the bowl of water. Wash each other's hands. Say the "Hand-washing Prayer" (on page 136, a copy of which has been placed next to the bowl of water). Share the feelings that emerged from the experience.

Think about the various kinds of people who make up your community.

Who are "the least" in your community.

Who are your enemies?

How have you reached out to them?

Think of someone you know who is good at reaching out to others. Describe this person to your small group.

Hand-washing Prayer

Loving God,
Remind *[name]* of the waters of *[his/her]* baptism.
Wash away everything that keeps *[him/her]* separated from you.
Bless all that *[his/her]* hands touch, and all that they make, and all that they do;
in the name of the Father, and of the Son, and of the Holy Spirit, Amen.

— Peter Bals (unpublished)

Christ has no body but yours,
no hands but yours,
no feet but yours.
Yours are the eyes through which
    Christ's compassion looks out
    on the world.
Yours are the feet with which
    he is to go about doing good.
And yours are the hands with which
    he is to bless us now.

— St. Teresa of Ávila

They Asked, "Who's My Neighbor?"

They asked, "Who's my neighbor and whom should I love;
    for whom should I do a good deed?"
Then Jesus related a story and said,
    "It's anyone who has a need, yes,
    anyone who has a need."

There once was a traveler set on by thieves
    who beat him and left him to die;
A priest and a Levite each saw him in pain;
    but they turned away and walked by, yes,
    they turned away and walked by.

A certain Samaritan then came along
    to bind up his wounds and give aid;
He took him to stay at an inn until well,
    and for all the service he paid, yes,
    for all the service he paid.

I know who's my neighbor and whom I should love,
    for whom I should do a good deed;
For Jesus made clear in the story he told,
    it's anyone who has a need, yes,
    anyone who has a need.

— Ruth Jannelle Wesson, *The New Century Hymnal*, #541

Within the Heart of God

In memory of Margaret, *1984-2016*

She was strikingly beautiful,
And a gentle soul really,
but one fired by rage at a life
of incomprehensible wounds.
She lived the only way she could
in order to survive lest she
like her half-sister, lose her mind.

She came from time to time,
needing help with something...
birthday gifts for her children in state custody,
hygiene or feminine products,
once it was shampoo for lice,
sometimes just wanting to talk.

This day she had left the hospital
against medical advice, swollen belly
eyes and skin the color of iodine.
Bee-line to the women's center,
hesitant and humble,
still in PJ's and slippers.

"One drink will kill you!" they had told her.
"For my kids, I don't want to die."
        she said to us.

A wad of prescriptions in hand,
given to keep her alive.
but no money to pay for them.
No food at her boarding room either.
we got the meds and some soup.
although she wouldn't need them.

Before good-bye "Do you want a hug?" I asked.
She took it and held on tight
as we rested a moment together
        totally vulnerable
within the heart of God.

She raised her head,
our eyes met for a long moment,
Hers so deep, mine so sad,
both holding back tears.
A whispered "We love you Margaret"
and let her go.

It was the best and only gift possible,
and the last...

She died the next day.

Pontius' Puddle

Through All the World, a Hungry Christ

Through all the world,
    a hungry Christ
must scavenge far for daily bread,
must beg the rich for crumb
    and crust—
we are the rich, the daily fed.
Beyond the church, a leper Christ
takes each untouchable by hand,
gives hope to those who have
    no trust,
whose stigma is our social brand.
In torture cell, a prisoner Christ
for justice and for truth must cry
to free the innocent oppressed
while we at liberty pass by.
We do not know you, beggar Christ,
we do not recognize your sores,
we do not see, for we are blind:
forgive us, touch us, make us yours.

— Shirley Erena Murray,
The New Century Hymnal, #587

Do all the good you can,

By all the means you can,

In all the ways you can,

In all the places you can,

At all the times you can,

To all the people you can,

As long as you can.

— John Wesley

Stupidity, weakness and disappointing narrowness are things that we must sometimes bear from those whom we must work amongst. But God bears them from us the whole time!

How often grace and love reach us through and in spite of our narrow ideas of Him, our cowardice and our refusals.... After that, can we dare to be critical or impatient of the smallness, weakness and absurdity of those to whom we are sent? Love teaches us that it is above all by admiration and generosity of spirit that we shall help and win them.

Admiration is so much more humbling to receive and so much more ennobling to give than any criticism can be. Christ never criticized anybody but the respectable and pious. With everybody else His thought went like a shaft of delight straight to something that He could admire. The love shown by the prostitute, the meekness shown by the publican, the faith of the centurion, the confidence of the penitent thief—all the things that irradiate and save humanity—love looks for these first, and one reason why Christ gives rest to the soul is that in His presence we are bound to love and not to criticize.

We should feel the same too towards the humble beauties of human character, all the things that Christ appeared to in love and which lept out in response to Him, and still do.

— Evelyn Underhill, *The Ways of the Spirit*

More love, more love, the heavens are blessing,
The angels are calling, O Zion: More Love!

If we love not each other in daily communion
How can we love God, whom we have not seen?

More love, more love, the heavens are blessing,
The angels are calling, O Zion: More Love!

— a Shaker song

> "Do random acts of kindness and senseless acts of beauty"
> vs. "Practice random acts of violence and senseless acts of cruelty."
>
> — Ann Hebert

Spirit of Jesus, If I Love My Neighbor

Spirit of Jesus, if I love my neighbor,
    out of my knowledge, leisure, power, or wealth,
open my mind to understand the anger of helplessness
    that hates my power to help.

And if, when I have answered need with kindness,
    my neighbor rises, wakened from despair,
open my heart to hear the cry for justice
    that struggles for the changes that I fear.

If I am hugging safety or possessions,
    uncurl my spirit, as your love prevails,
to join my neighbors, work for liberation,
    and find my freedom at the mark of nails.

    — Brian Wren, *The New Century Hymnal*, #590

Incident

Once riding in old Baltimore
Heart-filled, head-filled with glee,
I saw a Baltimorean
Keep looking straight at me.

Now I was eight and very small,
And he was no whit bigger,
And so I smiled, but he poked out
His tongue, and called me, "Nigger."

I saw the whole of Baltimore
From May until December;
Of all the things that happened there
That's all that I remember.

    — Countee Cullen

The Outcast

He walks with an uneven gait,
Barely noticeable, really.
He cannot type; one hand
Doesn't work too well.
His balance is poor; he hates
Edges, ledges, and heights.
He likes to do things slowly
And carefully, preferably
While sitting down.

Raised on the sound of laughter
Directed at people like himself,
He has learned to hold back until
He finds a time and space
In which to dwell.
He doesn't need a lot of time
Or a large space, but in this
Hurried age of crowded places,
He knows he is unwelcome.

    — Karen E. Gough, *Women's
Uncommon Prayers*, p. 262

Responding

Practicing Together:

• An old concept of "parish" was a geographic area surrounding a church building, a neighborhood. Identify such an area around your church, perhaps several square blocks or a certain mile radius. Imaginatively claim the territory as belonging to your faith community. You are responsible for what happens within its borders.

Walk around your church's neighborhood and interview people who live there.
Ask them questions about your church:
>   Do they know of it? How and why?
>   Have they ever been there? If not, why not?
>   If they have attended, how often?
>   If only once, why did they not come back?
>   What is their greatest wish for the neighborhood?

After collecting responses, discuss what you have learned.
>   Who are your neighbors?
>   What is the relationship between the nearby residents and your faith community?
>   Does your light shine in the neighborhood?
>   If your church were no longer present in the neighborhood, would anybody who lives
>   nearby know or care that you were gone?
>   How might you serve Christ in the neighborhood to meet the common good?
Extend the circle to your town or city, then to the world. Ask similar questions.

• Talk with local human service providers and schools to find out where there are gaps that need filling. Inventory your faith community's gifts and resources. Consider how you might match them with the identified situations. It may mean joining a Habitat for Humanity project (http://www.habitat.org), or committing volunteers to your local school, or providing literacy training, or supporting foster parenting, or opening an after-school safe space... or it may mean taking responsibility for finding others who can meet these needs.

- Learn about some international service organizations, like Episcopal Relief and Development (www.episcopalrelief.org), Church World Service (www.cwsglobal.org), and Heifer Project International (www.heifer.org). Talk about how you might become involved in these or similar programs.

Practicing at Home:

- Do you regularly give your time to a local or global outreach project? If you do, write about what you have learned from the experience. What made you choose this ministry? If you are not involved in outreach, why not? What might you do?

- Take daily notice of the news and consider what is happening locally and globally. Every day "pray the news" by holding the situations and people in God's light and love. Ask God to give you the wisdom and will to respond.

- Stop every time you hear a siren and pray for the rescuers and the rescued.

- How do you honor Christ in yourself? How do you balance the needs of self and neighbor? Have you ever felt "burned out" in your ministry?

- Volunteer in a soup kitchen or shelter and get to know the guests by name. Do some "Free Listening" there or on the street—listen without comment or judgement. Write about your experiences (www.urbanconfessional.org).

- In the United States we are increasingly a bilingual country of Spanish and English. Get to know our Spanish speaking neighbors and try to learn Spanish.

- Each morning, fill a bowl with water. As it fills, reflect on your life: your work, relationships, problems, joys, home, and other possessions. Receive your life, as it is, with openness. Take your bowl to the place established as an altar in your home, and—as you set the bowl down in its proper place on the altar—resolve to dedicate your life that day to the service of others. In the evening just before going to bed, return to the altar and the bowl of water and reflect on your day; then take the bowl outside and slowly pour the water out, letting the day go as the bowl empties.

— adapted from *My Grandfather's Blessings: Stories of Strength, Refuge, and Belonging* by Rachel Naomi Remen, p. 216

Closing Prayer

Sing again the Opening Song, "Ubi caritas," which was sung in the time of Gathering.
Take a moment to share thanksgivings and personal prayer needs.
Close with the following prayer and blessings.

Almighty God our heavenly Father, you declare your glory and show forth your handiwork in the heavens and in the earth: Deliver us in our various occupations from the service of self alone, that we may do the work you give us to do in truth and beauty and for the common good; for the sake of him who came among us as one who serves, your Son Jesus Christ our Lord, who lives and reigns with you and the Holy Spirit, one God, for ever and ever. Amen.

— "For Vocation in Daily Work," The Book of Common Prayer, p. 261

Most gracious Lord, whose appearing is as sure as the dawn: Come to us like the spring rains that water the earth, showering your blessings upon us and all whom you have made, that we may be strengthened by your love and may share that love with others; in the name of the Source, the Word, and the Spirit. Amen.

— Elizabeth Rankin Geitz, *Women's Uncommon Prayers*, p. 319

August 23

The parents are working on getting the chick to fish. They seem to be doing the drop-the- fish routine. It is wonderful to watch. When I went out this morning, they were in our cove—the chick is much bigger and is diving a lot now. There was a breeze, which blew me too close—an adult came right to the kayak underwater—first time I saw one swimming that way! You could tell it was coming—a stream of bubbles marked its path towards me. It surfaced just to my right and protested mightily, then swam under the boat, surfacing behind me. Time to move on! Hopefully got a couple pictures first.

Session Seven

Will you strive for justice and peace
among all people, and
respect the dignity of every human being?

Gathering

Scatter a collection of pictures of people from all over the world in the center of the room around the water bowl (Church World Service and Amnesty International calendars are two excellent sources for such photographs; stories accompany each photograph.)

There should be at least one picture for each person in the group.

OPENING SONG: Go Down, Moses

The setting for this spiritual is found in Lift Every Voice and Sing II, *#228.*

The verses of this song can be sung in a call-and-response fashion.

Sing it slowly. Everyone sings the refrain together.

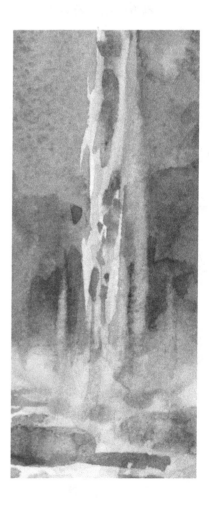

When Israel was in Egypt's land,
    let my people go;
oppressed so hard they could not stand,
    let my people go.

The Lord told Moses what to do,
    let my people go;
to lead the children of Israel through,
    let my people go.

They journeyed on at his command,
    let my people go;
and came at length to Canaan's land,
    let my people go.

Oh, let us all from bondage flee,
    let my people go;
and let us all in Christ be free,
    let my people go.

> *Refrain:*
> God down, Moses, way down in Egypt's land;
> tell old Pharaoh to let my people go.
>
> — Afro-American spiritual, *Lift Every Voice and Sing II, #228*

Exodus 14:19–31 Crossing the Red Sea

Ideally, this story is told, rather than read. If possible, invite a biblical storyteller to present the story.

Another technique is to have the group help tell the story by providing sound effects. Every time the name "Israel" or "Moses" is spoken, the group can cheer or say "yes!"; each time God is mentioned, they can say "ahh!"; for the words "Pharaoh" or "Egypt," they make a sound of disgust.

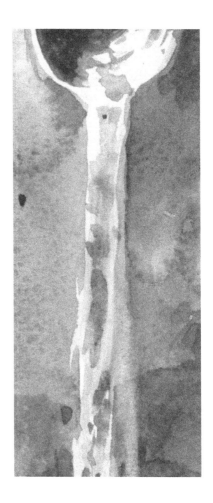

The angel of God who was going before the Israelite army
　　moved and went behind them;
　　　　and the pillar of cloud moved from in front of them and
　　　　took its place behind them.
It came between the army of Egypt and the army of Israel.
And so the cloud was there with the darkness, and it lit up
　　the night; one did not come near the other all night.

Then Moses stretched out his had over the sea.
The Lord drove the sea back by a strong east wind all night,
　　and turned the sea into dry land; and the waters were
　　divided.
The Israelites went into the sea on dry ground, the waters
　　forming a wall for them on their right and on their left.
The Egyptians pursued, and went into the sea after them,
　　all of Pharaoh's horses, chariots, and chariot drivers.
At the morning watch the Lord in the pillar of fire and cloud
　　looked down upon the Egyptian army, and threw the
　　Egyptian army into panic.
He clogged their chariot wheels so that they turned with difficulty.
The Egyptians said, "Let us flee from the Israelites,
　　for the Lord is fighting for them against Egypt."

Then the Lord said to Moses, "Stretch out your hand over the sea,
　　so that the water may come back upon the Egyptians,
　　upon their chariots and chariot drivers."
So Moses stretched out his hand over the sea,
　　and at dawn the sea returned to its normal depth.
As the Egyptians fled before it, the Lord tossed the Egyptians into the sea.
The waters returned and covered the chariots and the chariot drivers,
　　the entire army of Pharaoh that had followed them into the sea;
　　not one of them remained.

But the Israelites walked on dry ground through the sea,
    the waters forming a wall for them on their right and on their left.
Thus the LORD saved Israel that day from the Egyptians;
        and Israel saw the Egyptians dead on the seashore.
Israel saw the great work that the LORD did against the Egyptians.
So the people feared the LORD
        and believed in the LORD and in his servant Moses.

Psalm 114

Have everyone repeatedly, but not in unison, proclaim the opening Hallelujah!

Men and women then read the remaining verses responsively, by half verse as indicated by line spaces.

At the end, proclaim the Hallelujah again and in the same manner as before—repeatedly, but not in unison.

Hallelujah!

When Israel came out of Egypt,
the house of Jacob from a people of strange speech,

Judah became God's sanctuary
and Israel his dominion.

The sea beheld it and fled;
Jordan turned and went back.

The mountains skipped like rams,
and the little hills like young sheep.

What ailed you, O sea, that you fled?
O Jordan, that you turned back?

You mountains, that you skipped like rams?
you little hills like young sheep?

Tremble, O earth, at the presence of the Lord,
at the presence of the God of Jacob,

Who turned the hard rock into a pool of water
and flint-stone into a flowing spring.

Hallelujah!

For Personal, Silent Reflection

Imagine being in a massive crowd of refugees, fleeing a place of oppression. You have been on the run for days. God is your guide.
As if a single organism, the crowd surges toward freedom, which lies in the direction across a large sea. Miraculously, the waters of the sea part, allowing the people to cross to the other side. You turn to look back at those who are chasing you, but they have been swallowed up by the same sea you just crossed. For now at least, you are safe. You turn to the person closest to you

What do you say and do?

How do you feel about what has happened to you? To the Egyptians?

Now you face an unknown future.

What is your greatest hope? Your greatest fear?

What is your prayer to God?

The Lord's Prayer

Have each petition read by a different person.

The entire group responds with the italicized phrases.

Our Father, who art in heaven, slow to anger, and of great mercy,
lover of all the peoples of the earth,
Hallowed be thy Name.

Remind us that "all the nations are as nothing before thee,"
their governments but a shadow of passing age;
Thy kingdom come on earth.

Grant to thy children throughout all the world,
and especially to the leaders of the nations,
the gift of prayerful thought and thoughtful prayer;
that following the example of our Lord,
we may discern what is right, and do it;
Thy will be done on earth, as it is in heaven.

Help us to protect and to provide for all who are hungry and homeless,
especially those who are deprived of food and shelter,
family and friend, by the tragedy of war;
Give us this day our daily bread.

Forgive us for neglecting to "seek peace and pursue it,"
and finding ourselves in each new crisis,
more ready to make war than to make peace.
"We have not loved thee with our whole heart;
we have not loved our neighbors as ourselves";
Forgive us our trespasses, as we forgive those who trespass against us,

Let us not seek revenge, but reconciliation;
Let us not delight in victory, but in justice;
Let us not give ourselves up to pride, but to prayer;
Lead us not into temptation.

Be present to all thy children ravaged by war:
Be present to those who are killing and to those who are being killed;
Be present to the loved ones of those who are killing
and to the loved ones of those who are being killed;
Deliver us from evil.

Subdue our selfish desires to possess and to dominate,
and forbid us arrogance in victory;
For thine is the kingdom, and the power, and the glory, forever and ever.

Amen.

— Wendy Lyons, *Women's Uncommon Prayers*, p. 280

Collect

Almighty God, who created us in your own image:
Grant us grace fearlessly to contend against evil
and to make no peace with oppression;
and, that we may reverently use our freedom,
help us to employ it in the maintenance of justice
in our communities and among the nations,
to the glory of your holy Name; through Jesus Christ our Lord,
who lives and reigns with you and the Holy Spirit,
one God, now and for ever. Amen.

— "For Social Justice," The Book of Common Prayer, p. 260

Sharing

MY MOTHER ARRIVED in this country in 1947 with two suitcases that together weighed only forty pounds. She spoke no English. Six years later, after having put herself through business school, she married. During and after the Hungarian revolution of 1956, she frequently gave presentations to community and school groups about the trauma in her homeland under Communist rule, where her sister and other relatives still lived.

My mother once told me about the day she stopped hating the Russians for what they did to her homeland. It was in 1980, on her first trip back to Hungary after more than 30 years away. While walking one day in Budapest, she came across a memorial to Russian fathers, husbands, and sons who died—as Russian propaganda would have it—"liberating" Hungary. But instead of getting angry, Mom said she suddenly realized in her heart that Russian mothers had sons, too... sons just like her own son, Mark, who had just reached draftable age.

When the Iran hostage crisis happened in 1979-81, Mom was one of many members of our church who rang the steeple bells each day at noon as a reminder of, and witness to, the injustice of the situation, and as a call to prayer vigilance. The day the hostages were released, Inauguration Day, 1981, she was the one appointed to ring the bell. The time alone in the church that day brought her to reflect on her experiences of war, her life as a political refugee, and on her sorrow over the regime in her homeland. It brought back a flood of feelings which she expressed in a meditation she wrote for our church newsletter:

> To have the hostages freed that day was almost more joy than I could stand. During those agonizingly long months, as we took turns ringing our church bell, I had to participate whenever I could. I rang lovingly and faithfully for those fifty-two Americans; but in my heart, I also rang for all my fellow human beings all over the world that do not enjoy the freedoms that we know here. I especially rang the bell for my beloved family and friends who are in bondage in Hungary. I often felt as if the prayer on the bulletin board in the bell tower was written for me: "God, as the bell rings forth day by day over this free land, send the strength of your Holy Spirit to comfort and uphold all those in bondage."
>
> While I rang, I remembered my own experiences during the war in Europe. I have been almost able to forget it all, but incidents such as the Iran hostage situation bring memories

back. I know the cold terror of living in constant fear of losing one's life or the lives of loved ones. The line in the Lord's Prayer, "Give us this day our daily bread," has quite a meaning for me, for there were times when even a slice of unleavened bread was a treat. I still consider bathing in a full tub of hot water something very special, and I cannot slip between two clean sheets without being grateful for them. As those men and women returned, you perhaps were rejoicing with them in generalities. I could identify with a thousand different things they might have experienced and felt.

No one goes through an ordeal such as that and remains the same. The fifty-two who return are not the same as the day they were taken. Their experience has changed us, too, individually and collectively. It certainly has made me aware all over again of how fortunate I am to be living here. I pray that this experience may continue to echo in our hearts in the weeks, months, and even years to come.

Some ten years later, we entered into yet another conflict, this time in Iraq. The night our attacks began, I found my Mom standing in the middle of her kitchen, watching the live broadcast of the events on CNN. Upon hearing the air raid sirens, she looked at me in horror and repeatedly said, "My knees won't stop shaking!" The experience of war was happening for her all over again. It was as if she was waiting for the next bomb to drop on *us*.

In the early 1990s, I had the opportunity to spend a year in Hungary as a mission volunteer. Being there was a remarkable experience of getting to know Mom's early life and my cultural roots. It also helped me understand her passionate commitments to justice and peace. Those commitments are becoming my own as I ask myself "How can I continue to hate? How can I learn to not hate?" Although I don't know what the answer is, I do know that Jesus taught another way and that like many, I am struggling to find it.

HAVING GROWN UP in a mostly white rural Ohio farming community, the civil rights movement, while in the news and very much in my parent's consciousness, seemed very far away. The most direct experience was the recovery of hidden tunnels and rooms in town that had been part of the Underground Railroad. There were also family stories of my grandmother in Delaware, writing letters to the editor about the unfair treatment of "Negroes."

For high school I attended a small, southern, Episcopal girl's boarding school—Stuart Hall, class of 1973. The school was named for J. E. B. Stuart, a Confederate war general. His portrait, confederate battle flag, and other memorabilia were proudly displayed in the front parlor.

Given that setting, it amazes me now that we were given books to read by Black writers like

W. E. B. Du Bois and Frederick Douglass. We may have even read *The Autobiography of Malcom X*. That educational effort might have been because the first two African American girls to attend that school were admitted, on full scholarship, to my class. Perhaps the administration was going to great lengths to make the transition to integration work.

I also remember a famous Black man was invited to lecture once. My memory is that it was Alex Haley, although the publishing of his book *Roots* was not until 1976, the movie a bit later. We met with him for a time of Q&A in that parlor where General Stuart was so present. The irony of that contradiction did not surface in any of our minds. Regretfully, I can recall the name of only one of the two African American girls who were my high school classmates. My memory of her is mostly that we both had a part in our class play, and as alumni we were notified of her untimely and tragic death a number of years back. I have no clue about the other student of color.

However imperfect it was, I am grateful for those experiences. They began expanding my awareness of racism.

Years later, my racism hit me smack in the face. I was attending the General Convention of the Episcopal Church in 1991, held in Phoenix, Arizona. There had been much debate about the location that year, and whether or not the Episcopal Church should boycott the city and move the convention elsewhere, as did the National Football League in moving the Super Bowl from Phoenix to Los Angeles. Three decades after the civil rights movement, the issue at hand was that the Arizona

had twice voted not to recognize the Martin Luther King Jr. holiday as a paid holiday.

The decision was made to keep the General Convention in Phoenix, but while there, to do all we could to raise awareness about racism. Several resolutions on the topic were presented and passed, speakers addressed the topic, and Bible studies focused on racism, as did one Convention Eucharist.

We were all seated at the same tables that were used for the daily morning scripture conversations. At the great Thanksgiving, I looked over my shoulder at the large group of clergy who were organized to bring the bread and wine to each table. They each held a chalice and paten and after the consecration, they were to distribute the elements to the tables.

This was about 12 years after the Episcopal Church had opened ordination to women. Startled by what I saw I spontaneously whispered with exasperation to my neighbor… "Oh my, they are all men!" To which she, an African American woman, replied, "Yes, and they are all white."

Yes, indeed… they were all men… and they were all white. But I had only noticed half the problem even after over a week of focusing on racism: I felt so embarrassed as I quietly wept.

Between then and now, as repeated situations have periodically called us to consciousness, the church has offered anti-racism trainings. I have participated in more than I can count. From time to time, legislators are compelled to debate and resolve. Even so, murders and accusations continue to be inflicted on our black and brown brothers and sisters. Indigenous peoples still have to fight for their rights to land, health care, and recognition. Institutional systems of oppression and white privilege remain largely in place, economic disparities grow, and equal representation is a long way off—even in the Church. Why?

That is the reality of racism. For centuries, it has been so very ingrained in our psyches, that unconsciously, we look, but just do not see. Only now are we thinking deeply about what the Civil War symbols that we so proudly displayed, have said to people of color. Maybe we are finally at a tipping point. With social media, we can no longer so easily avoid seeing the realities of injustice. They come to us immediately rather than only in newspapers, weeks, days or months later (if at all). In response to recent events, there are protests and the old symbols like Confederate statues and flags are coming down. Setting things right will be like slowly peeling back an onion, one layer at a time. Sometimes it will, and should make us weep in lament and contrition, especially those of us who have benefitted from the status quo. May this time bring deep change and renewed life for us all.

This is How We Live

— by Shatha Farah

This story—which was submitted for the Lent 2002 edition of Treasure Magazine, *the mission resource published by the Episcopal Church Office of Children's Ministries and Christian Education—is one of several written by children of the Diocese of Jerusalem to children in the Episcopal Church. Shatha Farah was a ninth-grader in a school in Gaza when this letter was written. Her original text has been retained here with only minor editing.*

AS THE SUN FADED into the sea, leaving a sky filled with sunset colors in every corner of the heavens. The clock had struck. It is six o'clock. I was sitting with my mother, and my two sisters in the living room. My dad was doing some work in the bedroom. The house was calm, but not for so long, at once we all heard a new sound coming through our ears. We trembled and ran to the kitchen, after a few seconds the electricity went off, we heard that sound again, my heart beats were running fast, faster than the lightning, and many questions flashed in my mind. I was living a moment of wonder filled with fear.

While my brain was hunting answers for the questions that have been asked, I was moving with my terrified soul, and with my family towards the hall, we sat there on the floor, watching the light of the bombs on the walls, hearing the thunder of crashes, the buzzing of the planes that were flying above the frightened city. I was holding my father tightly, shaking and praying. The hours of the night went slow. No stars were in the sky. Tears took place in my eyes, and the joy was not painted in the hearts as it used to be. Only pictures of sadness were seen. The bombing was finished.

I went to sleep wondering if I am going to see the shining sun again or not! Since that night I met the real fear. I imagined death surrounding me from each side. I survived but in each time when I remember that sound, it tears me up and brings back to me the memories of that scary day. I remember some scenes from the last few months. My sister who came in the beginning of the Intifada back with a master degree and for more than 6

For Small Group Discussion

Describe the most peaceful person you know.

What is it about him/her that makes you feel this way.

Do you have a hero? Describe him/her.

When have you felt that your dignity was trampled upon?

What did you do?

Describe a time when you served as a peacemaker.

Describe a time when you witnessed an injustice.

What was your response?

Choose one of the photographs in the center of the room. Focus on the faces, especially the eyes. Imagine what the person in the photograph might tell you if he/she were in the room with you. Share the story you imagined in the small group.

months she has not got a job. My parents who prayed a lot for being at the graduation party of their elder son couldn't reach the airport. My brother who was trying all the time to draw the picture of how his friend died. Not only my family that suffered, but also all of the Palestinian families. If we visit each house we will find, many houses that have an unemployed father! Another houses that have 10 hungry mouths. Or sick bodies, or may be have not enough clothing to keep the children warm

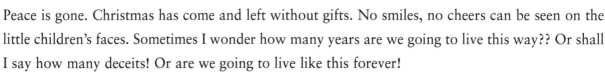

Weakness, no safety, demonstrations, no freedom, no justice, that's how we live.

All the dreams of the future have been deleted! Peace is gone. Christmas has come and left without gifts. No smiles, no cheers can be seen on the little children's faces. Sometimes I wonder how many years are we going to live this way?? Or shall I say how many deceits! Or are we going to live like this forever!

All I can do is keep on praying for the day when the rainbow of peace will appear in the sky of Palestine once again, announcing peace after a tragic hurricane. I add to this saying that freedom will be here as long as the hope is living in us. So let's keep on the hope....

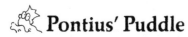

Pontius' Puddle

SOMETIMES I'D LIKE TO ASK GOD WHY HE ALLOWS POVERTY, FAMINE AND INJUSTICE WHEN HE COULD DO SOMETHING ABOUT IT.

WHAT'S STOPPING YOU?

I'M AFRAID GOD MIGHT ASK ME THE SAME QUESTION.

© Joel Kauffmann

Reflecting

Scripture

Exodus 3	Moses at the burning bush
Exodus 14, 15	The Exodus from Egypt

(Exodus 15:1–18, Song of Moses; Exodus 15:20–22, Song of Miriam)

Psalm 146	Praise for God's help and justice
Isaiah 11:1–9	The peaceable kingdom
Isaiah 28:17–19	Justice the line, and righteousness the plummet
Isaiah 32:1–8	Government with justice
Isaiah 43:16–21	I am about to do a new thing
Amos 5:14–15, 24	Let justice roll down like waters
Micah 6:6–8	What God requires
Matthew 7:12	The "golden rule"

(Luke 6:31)

Matthew 18:23–35	Parable of the unforgiving servant
Matthew 20:1–16	Laborers in the vineyard
Luke 1:46–55	Song of Mary
Luke 4:16–30	Jesus is rejected at Nazareth

(also Isaiah 61)

Luke 6:27–36	Love for enemies

(Matthew 5:43–48)

Luke 16:19–31	Rich man and Lazarus
Colossians 3:1–17	New life in Christ

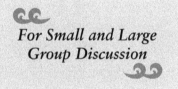

For Small and Large Group Discussion

Refer to the scripture selections. Choose one or two that speak to you and discuss them.

What word or phrase jumps out at you?

What does the passage say to you?

What is it calling you to do?

Consider any of the suggested hymns that relate to your conversation. Read over the Prayer Book selections and comments.

What light do they shed on your conversation?

Hymns

The Hymnal 1982

    In Bethlehem a newborn boy, #246
    Go forth for God, #347
    All who love and serve your city, #571
    Weary of all trumpeting, #572
    Father eternal, #573
    O God of love, O King of peace, #578
    Lord, make us servants of your peace, #593
    O day of peace that dimly shines, #597
    What does the Lord require, #605
    O God of every nation, #607
    Dona nobis pacem, #712
    Shalom chaverim, #714

Wonder, Love, and Praise

    The desert shall rejoice, #722
    Isaiah the prophet has written of old, #723
    Gracious Spirit, #782
    We are marching in the light of God, #787
    Peace before us, #791
    Come now, O Prince of Peace, #795
    You shall cross the barren desert, #811

Lift Every Voice and Sing II

    Wade in the water, #143
    Down by the riverside, #210
    Oh, freedom! #225
    We shall overcome, #227

The Book of Common Prayer

The Catechism:
    The Old Covenant, pp. 847–847
    The Ten Commandments, pp. 847–848
Prayers for the World:
    "For the Human Family," p. 815
    "For Peace," p. 815
    "For Peace Among the Nations," p. 816
    "For our Enemies," p. 816
Prayers for the Social Order:
    "For Social Justice," p. 823
    "In Times of Conflict," p. 824
    "For the Oppressed," p. 826
Prayers for Family and Personal Life:
    "A Prayer attributed to St. Francis," p. 833

Shortly after the opening of the Berlin Wall, my mother had a chance to visit Berlin. The fall of the political system it represented, that had kept her own family captive in Hungary, was something she never thought she would see in her lifetime. To this day, she keeps a fragment of the Berlin Wall in a small glass box in her china cabinet. While in Berlin, Mom took a photo of some graffiti on a piece of the wall. One read, "Many small people, who in many small places, do many small things, can alter the face of the world." She enlarged the photo for me for Christmas that year. It hangs over my desk.

Unlike the previous vow, this one—to strive for justice and peace—is more often acted out in the public sphere, en masse. The vow is about personal forgiveness, taken to the community level. We must speak truth about injustice to the world, maintain a listening and pastoral presence, and become advocates in the body politic, for the greater good of all. In her book *Fashion Me a People,* Maria Harris talks about our call to be Christ-like. She reminds us that, if we are to follow our model, Jesus—who is prophet, priest, and king—then we must be prophetic, priestly, and political.

The hitch is that there is no exception to the rule in the vow. Notice the qualifiers. It says we must strive for justice and peace among *all* people and respect the dignity of *every* human being. That includes terrorists, unethical politicians, ruthless business executives, criminals, and drug dealers. How is it possible to do justice while still respecting the dignity of those who do not do justice? How do we not demonize the "other" in situations of conflict? My father's lesson to his children was to remind us constantly not to judge anyone until we "walk a mile in that person's shoes."

We may need to look, first, at ourselves when we see injustice. Jesus warned those who were condemning a woman to death that only the person who is without sin should cast the first stone. Our sins may be outright—things we have done; or they may be subtler—things left undone, things left unsaid, complicity. It is not easy, this striving for justice and peace and dignity for all. Perhaps that is why this vow uses the verb "strive," a word choice that enables us to stay prayerful and be grounded and to just keep trying.

A Prayer of Anti-Racism
(after Ibram X. Kendi)

God of all Goodness,
we refuse to give up hope
in Your vision of a just world:

Cultivate in us a stubborn belief
in the possibility of an equitable society,
despite our nation's history.

Guide us to respond to human differences
without fear, relating to one another as equals,
   seeking a common future,
seeking communion.

Inspire in us the tenacity
to explore the habits of thinking,
as well as the practices and policies
that deny human freedom and flourishing.

Give us strength to do the work
of eliminating racial inequity,
in all its intersections and manifestations,
one racist policy at a time,
one power change at a time.

Accompany us, we pray,
in our striving to be anti-racist and,
from this day forward,
bless our struggles to oppose
all forms of racism
in our systems and in ourselves.
Amen.

— Kathy Bozzuti-Jones, 2020,
   used by permission of the author

For Small Group Discussion

Think of one person with whom you experience discord.

What are the steps you might take to find a just and lasting peace with this person?

Name a current local or global conflict that concerns you.

How do boundaries and boundary-keeping break the peace?
Make the peace?

What is the place of the individual in a group conflict?

What does scripture say to these situations?

Read Luke 4:14–30.

How have you been, or might you be, Christ-like (prophetic, priestly, political)?

Jesus is called "Prince of Peace." He paid the price for peace and justice with his life.

How have you contributed to injustice or discord?

How have you contributed to peace and justice?

What did this contribution cost you?

Where in your daily life can you make peace?

*Reflectively read one or two of the following quotes.
What is your response?*

A Pastoral Letter

How then, can we continually receive the eucharistic Christ and leave untouched or unchanged any bitter or hardened prejudice against any member of any race of people? We tell ourselves that we mean no harm to anyone. Yet at the same time, we repeat the cheap racial joke, we make the ill-advised remark, we indulge in self-righteous anger in the home—all these plant the seed of a whole new generation of prejudice in our children. It seems so unimportant, so trivial. But multiply it by thousands and it becomes a cancer of sinful attitudes which sickens and weakens the body of the church. Small wonder that men ask how can it be the *same* Christ that we love....

Liturgy understood as *the worship* of the church and social action understood as *the work* of the church are part, one of the other. Liturgy which does not move its participants to social action is mere ceremonialism; social action which does not find its source in the liturgy is mere humanitarianism.

> — Richard Cardinal Cushing; as quoted
> in *A Sourcebook about Liturgy*,
> Liturgy Training Publications, p. 15

I Sit and Look Out

I sit and look out upon all the sorrows of the world,
And upon all oppression and shame,
I hear secret convulsive sobs from young men
   at anguish with themselves,
Remorseful after deeds done,
I see in low life the mother misused by her children,
Dying, neglected, gaunt, desperate,
I see the wife misused by her husband,
I see the treacherous seducer of young women,
I mark the ranklings of jealousy and unrequited love
   attempted to be hid,
I see these sights on the earth,
I see the working of battle, pestilence, tyranny,
I see martyrs and prisoners,
I observe a famine at sea,
I observe the sailors casting lots who shall be kill'd
   to preserve the lives of the rest,
I observe the slights and degradations cast by
   arrogant persons
Upon laborers, the poor, and upon negroes, and
   the like:
All these—all the meanness and agony without end
I sitting look out upon,
See, hear, and am silent.

> — Walt Whitman

Be my refuge

Let me find a home in you
Give me your tired,
Give me the courage to welcome
And serve the tired...
the really, really tired

Be my refugee
Find a home in me
Your poor,
Because poverty is
One ugly wrecking machine
Mother Teresa, *Ora pro nobis*

Your huddled masses yearning
To breathe free
Made to love and to be loved
Give me eyes to see and
A heart free enough to
Make a space for you

Wretched refuse of your teeming shore
Come by here
O Refugee God
Send these, the homeless, the tempest-
Tossed to me, I lift my lamp beside
the Golden door!

The same door where God stands
And knocks
The same door where Love
bade me welcome
Open unto me the door
Of my own heart

> — Mark Francisco Bozzuti-Jones, poem and
> photo used by permission of author

Quotations from the King National Historic Site

When evil men plot,
  good men must plan.
When evil men burn and bomb,
  good men must build and bind.
When evil men shout ugly words of hatred,
  good men must commit themselves
  to the glories of love.
Where evil men would seek to perpetuate an
  unjust status quo, good men must seek
  to bring into being a real order of justice.

A religion true to its nature must also be concerned
about man's social conditions.... Any religion that
professes to be concerned with the souls of men and is
not concerned with the slums that damn them, the
economic conditions that strangle them, and the social
conditions that cripple them is a dry-as-dust religion.

> — Martin Luther King Jr.

Give me your tired, your poor,
your huddled masses
yearning to breathe free,
the wretched refuse
of your teeming shore.

Send these, the homeless,
tempest-tost to me,
I lift my lamp
beside the golden door!

> — Emma Lazarus, from
> "The New Colossus"

Many small people, who in many small places,
do many small things, can alter the face of the world.
— from a photo my mom took of the Berlin Wall in 1989

Love the dispossessed, all those who, living amid human injustice,
thirst after justice. Jesus had special concern for them.
Have no fear of being disturbed by them.
— from the Rule of Taizé

Send us now into the world in peace,
and grant us strength and courage
to love and serve you
with gladness and singleness of heart;
through Christ our Lord, Amen.
— Postcommunion Prayer, The Book of
Common Prayer, p. 365

Seven Deadly social sins:
    Politics without principle
    Wealth without work
    Commerce without morality
    Pleasure without conscience
    Education without character
    Science without humanity
    Worship without sacrifice
— Mohandas Gandhi

When we wonder as adults whether we are loved, we know that we belong to God. But we also belong to the world. We are baptized into solidarity with the world in Christ at the level of deepest danger. In that sense, baptism is always a precarious political act. Because we have been baptized, we are linked to the sufferings of the world for which Christ died. Because we have been baptized, our hospitality always has room for the weak and the vulnerable.
— Herbert Anderson and Edward Foley,
Mighty Stories, Dangerous Rituals:
Weaving Together the Human and
the Divine, p. 73

Never doubt that a small group of thoughtful committed citizens
can change the world: Indeed, it's the only thing that ever has!
— Margaret Mead

First they came for the Socialists, and I did not speak out because I was not a socialist. Then they came for the trade unionists, and I did not speak out because I was not a trade unionist. Then they came for the Jews, and I did not speak out because I was not a Jew. Then they came for me, and there was no one left to speak for me.

— Martin Niemöller

Think globally, act locally.
— popular slogan

Hine Ma Tov

Hine ma tov uma naim
Shevet achim gam yahad.
Hine ma tov uma naim
Shevet achim gam yahad.

Hine matov
she vet achim gam ya chad.
Hine matov
she vet achim gam ya chad.

(Here is what's good, nothing's better,
Brothers who dwell together.)

— a round based on Psalm 133 that is sung at Passover (a recording can be found on *God Help Us* by the Miserable Offenders)

The second word in the compound noun meaning "respect" is a word that might be rendered in English as "heavy" or "important." This ideogram shows a person balancing a yoke while steadily grounded. One can almost imagine the weights on the ends of the yoke in the calligraphic movement.

Responding

Practicing Together:

• Look at some charcoal drawings of Käthe Kollwitz. What feelings do they evoke in you? Learn about her witness to peace and justice through her life and art during WWI and WWII. Copy one of the drawings with charcoal; draw freehand if possible, or use tracing paper. Do this without speaking, with some appropriate music playing in the background. Post the drawings in your meeting room.

— an activity learned form Maria Harris

• Pray the prayer attributed to St. Francis (BCP, p. 833). Or sing it using hymn #593 in *The Hymnal 1982*. Discuss how you are—and how you could be—an instrument of God's peace. Make a list of current local and global situations in which there is discord among people, in which, perhaps, conflict or even violence has erupted. Can you identify the sources of the conflict? Whose dignity is at risk? What are the related injustices? Discuss how your church community might be an instrument of peace in the situation.

• Make a list of injustices throughout history. Consider especially the situation of the indigenous peoples of the earth.

> What issues have been left unspoken?
> What has been done to rectify the wrongs?
> Is any form of restitution called for?
> What would be the cost?

• There is a social movement toward "restorative justice" rather than "retributive justice." What is the difference? Discuss how your community might contribute to bringing justice. What would it take to completely restore justice?

• Look at a print of a painting by Edward Hicks, *The Peaceable Kingdom,* and notice particularly the small inset scene of two groups of people making peace. Read Isaiah 11:1–9, and other Isaiah passages on the scripture list. What images for peace are expressed? What is your image for peace?

• Learn about international justice and advocacy organizations such as Doctors Without Borders (www.doctorswithoutborders.org) or Amnesty International (www.amnesty-usa.org) and other social justice organizations. Invite someone from those organizations to speak with your group.

- Make a pilgrimage to any of the following sites: The National Holocaust Museum, the National Museum of African American History and Culture, or the National Museum of the Native American in Washington, DC. Or visit the United Nations building in New York. In Alabama, go to the Legacy Museum and Memorial for Peace and Justice and the Civil Rights Memorial in Montgomery that focus on the history of enslavement, lynching, and incarceration, or the Civil Rights Institute and 16th St. Baptist Church in Birmingham. If you can't travel that far, many states have similar museums. Or you can at least visit websites and learn about the museums that way.

- Join the Episcopal Public Policy Network (www.episcopalchurch.org/office-government-relations). Research their "Action Alerts." Pick one policy issue that you will follow and become involved with.

- Can war ever be "just"? The answer to that question has been debated for centuries. Read about the "just war theory," and read biblical passages about waging peace. Struggle with the gray areas. How do you respond to this debate? Have you ever reversed your opinion of, and feelings about, a particular military action? Talk with someone with whom you strongly disagree on this issue. Try to find common ground. If there is a military base near you, invite a military chaplain to speak with your group. What would you do if you were drafted? Why?

- Listen to Britten's *War Requiem*. This requiem was commissioned to celebrate the consecration in 1962 of the rebuilt Coventry Cathedral, which was destroyed during World War II. Britten wrote the parts of the soldiers for Peter Pears and Dietrich Fischer-Dieskau—one English singer and one German singer. The text of *War Requiem* is by Wilfred Owen. Read some of Owen's poetry ("Dulce et Decorum Est" is his most famous poem). The young poet served as a soldier in World War I and was killed in battle just a week prior to the Armistice.

Practicing at Home:

- Plot the hours of your waking day lengthwise across a piece of graph paper; make such a sheet for each day of the week. In one color of marker, shade in blocks of time when you feel most peaceful. In another color, shade in the blocks of time when you feel the least peaceful. Can you identify anything in particular that set your mood? Are you satisfied with the balance? If not, why not? How might you bring your day into better balance?

- Read a biography of one of the Nobel Peace Prize winners. Or read a memoir of a Holocaust survivor (Elie Wiesel's book *Night* is one good example). What do you learn from them about respecting the dignity of others?

- Meditate on Psalms 133 and 146. Write your own psalm, one that expresses your vision for justice and peace. Or draw your vision.

- Keep a list of places in your community and in the world that are struggling with conflict. Bookmark stories you see online about those situations and hold them in your daily prayers.

- Do some research and find out who were the indigenous inhabitants of the land on which you now live. Learn about them and the history of what happened. Honor the tribe or nation by recognizing the reality of the land as stolen. An app called Native Land will help: native-land.ca/maps. In Maine, the Council of Churches led by Quakers and Episcopalians is very involved in restoration and restitution work with the Wabanaki Confederacy (www.mainewabanakireach.org).

- Find out how to become an ally for marginalized people in your community. Listen to their stories. Show up for them as a shield or advocate when needed. Speak up and challenge when you hear racist jokes or stereotypes spoken. Befriend those who are different from you and take time to listen to their life stories.

- Learn about the justice system and incarceration complex. Reach out to organizations that help with prisoner re-entry. You might consider writing someone who is incarcerated or visit them before release so you can be part of a support system when they are released. Add their first names to your prayer list at home and at church.

- If you are Caucasian, learn about the theory of "white privilege." Make a list of the hidden ways you have been supported through life and been benefitted by family, education, society, culture, history.

- Read. Start with the poems of Langston Hughes like *Let America Be America Again*, and writings of Frederick Douglass, especially his Fourth of July Speech. Read them aloud, slowly. Do the same with speeches of Dr. Martin Luther King Jr. and other historic leaders and writers of the civil rights movement. Hear them as if for the first time. Read the writing of James Baldwin and watch the documentary about him called "I Am Not Your Negro." Immerse yourself in novels by writer like Toni Morrison and the poetry of Maya Angelou. Read biographies about Harriet Tubman, Ida B. Wells, and Sojourner Truth, along with later civil rights leaders and any books about the civil rights struggle. Organize book groups around these readings. With younger people, read and discuss books like *Freedom Over Me: Eleven Slaves, Their Lives and Dreams Brought to Life* by Ashley Bryan. There are many more books and videos. Your local public librarian can direct you.

- Many of the Saints in our liturgical calendar were witnesses for justice and peace and respecting the dignity of all human beings. Pay particular attention not only to Martin Luther King Jr. (January 15) but also to Jonathan Daniels (August 14); Absalom Jones (February 13); the Liberators and Prophets—Elizabeth Cady Stanton, Amelia Bloomer, Sojourner Truth, Harriet Tubman (July 20); and Dietrich Bonhoeffer (April 9).

- Read the poem "The New Colossus" by Emma Lazarus that is on the Statue of Liberty. Gather photos of refugees at our southern border and other places around the world. Begin to wonder why they left their homeland. If you know a first-generation immigrant, ask if they would be willing to share their story. Pray the poem above by Mark Fransisco Bozzuti-Jones called "Be

My Refuge." Connect with Episcopal Migration Ministries to learn more about how you can help. https://episcopalmigrationministries.org. Learn about the Episcopal Church global partnerships and get involved in your diocesan partnership: www.episcopalchurch.org/ministries/globalpartnerships.

Closing Prayer
Sing again the Opening Song, "Go down, Moses," which was sung in the time of Gathering.
Take a moment to share thanksgivings and personal prayer needs.
Close with the following prayer and blessing.

Eternal God, who led your ancient people into freedom by a pillar of cloud by day and a pillar of fire by night: Grant that we who walk in the light of your presence may rejoice in the liberty of the children of God; through Jesus Christ our Lord. Amen.

— collect for Evening Worship in Easter Season, The Book of Common Prayer, p. 111

O Holy Spirit, love within: kindle within us the flame of your burning passion, that we may work without ceasing for justice and peace on earth, and at length may attain to your love that never ends; in the name of the Source, the Word, and the Spirit. Amen.

— Elizabeth Rankin Geitz, *Women's Uncommon Prayers,* Proper 15, p. 319

August 29

Got up early this morning. Made an excursion to the last lake in our chain—Purgatory Pond. Never been there. Quite a haul in the kayak. It is a smaller lake, with no motorboats, so is wonderfully quiet. Saw another loon family there—one chick. This one is much bigger. Must have hatched earlier. That makes a total of six on our chain this year. Not bad!

Much to see. Two loon chicks paddling around together in Woodbury Pond, with no adults in sight. A group of five adults swimming in the cove by the beach. Later a group of seven flying over head, the lead one hooting. Have never seen that before.

Pre-migration rituals—hanging out together and stretching wings? Also saw a heron and an osprey. The season is turning—crickets—a late summer sound. We all must soon leave for the winter.

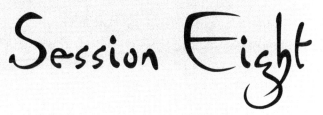

Session Eight

Will you cherish and protect creation?

Gathering

Place a collection of small, smooth river rocks in the bowl of water. You can purchase bags of them at craft stores. There should be at least one small rock for each person.

Lay small bunches of branches from a conifer or small-leaf bush around the bowl, one bunch for each person.

OPENING SONG: Peace Is Flowing Like a River

This is a simple, well-known song. It can be found in the hymnal, Gather *(GIA Publications, #306). As an alternative, sing "Peace before us," in* Wonder, Love, and Praise, *#791. In either song, you can produce additional verses by replacing the word "peace" with other words: love, joy, hope, justice, faith, prayer, spirit, etc. If you prefer to speak, rather than sing, the words, you might play a recording of flowing water in the background.*

Peace is flowing like a river
Flowing out from you and me,
Flowing out into the desert,
Setting all the captives free.

— adaptation of Psalm 127 by Carey Landry

EZEKIEL 36:25–28

Have a different person read each of the thirteen separate lines.

I will sprinkle clean water upon you,
    and you shall be clean from all your uncleannesses,
    and from all your idols I will cleanse you.
A new heart I will give you,
    and a new spirit I will put within you;
    and I will remove from your body the heart of stone
    and give you a heart of flesh.
I will put my spirit within you,
    and make you follow my statutes
    and be careful to observe my ordinances.

Then you shall live in the land that I gave to your ancestors;
    and you shall be my people,
    and I will be your God.

JOHN 7:37–38

*Have one person read the part of the narrator, another person
speak the words of Jesus.*

On the last day of the festival, the great day,
    while Jesus was standing there, he cried out,
        "Let anyone who is thirsty come to me,
        and let the one who believes in me drink.
        As the scripture has said,
            'Out of the believer's heart
            shall flow rivers of living water.'"

ISAIAH 35

*Have half the group read together the first set of verses
(up to the first line space).*

*The other half of the group reads the second set of verses
(up to the second line space).*

Everyone reads the third set of verses.

The wilderness and the dry land shall be glad,
    the desert shall rejoice and blossom;
    like the crocus it shall blossom abundantly,
    and rejoice with joy and singing.
The glory of Lebanon shall be given to it,
    the majesty of Carmel and Sharon.
They shall see the glory of the LORD,
    the majesty of our God.
Strengthen the weak hands,
    and make firm the feeble knees.
Say to those who are of a fearful heart,
        "Be strong, do not fear!
        Here is your God.
        He will come with vengeance,
        with terrible recompense.
        He will come and save you."

For Personal, Silent Reflection

Jesus has been at a week-long Jewish
  festival that commemorates the
  wilderness wanderings. Each day, water
  was carried from the Pool of Siloam to
  the temple as a reminder of the water
  that flowed from a rock to quench the
  thirst of the people in the desert. Jesus
  has been teaching in the temple. His
  words and acts astonish and anger the
  crowds. Everyone is confused. On the last
  "great day" of the festival, Jesus cries out
  that all who are thirsty may come to him;
  then he recites a scriptural reference to
  rivers of living water. His words make
  some believe that Jesus is a prophet, or
  even the Messiah. Others become
  convinced they should arrest him.

Think about Jesus's words about rivers of
  living water.

What is your greatest thirst?

Does living water flow from your heart?
  How do you know it?

Remember the words of Ezekiel.

From what would you like to be cleansed?

What is the deepest desire of your heart?

When has your heart felt like stone?

When has it been soft, like flesh?

Then the eyes of the blind shall be opened,
    and the ears of the deaf unstopped;
    then the lame shall leap like a deer,
    and the tongue of the speechless sing for joy.
For waters shall break forth in the wilderness,
    and streams in the desert;
    the burning sand shall become a pool,
    and the thirsty ground springs of water;
    the haunt of jackals shall become a swamp,
    the grass shall become reeds and rushes.

A highway shall be there,
    and it shall be called the Holy Way;
    the unclean shall not travel on it,
    but it shall be for God's people;
    no traveler, not even fools, shall go astray.
No lion shall be there,
    nor shall any ravenous beast come up on it;
    they shall not be found there,
    but the redeemed shall walk there.
And the ransomed of the LORD shall return,
    and come to Zion with singing;
    everlasting joy shall be upon their heads;
    they shall obtain joy and gladness,
    and sorrow and sighing shall flee away.

The Lord's Prayer

Heavenly Father, heavenly Mother,
Holy and blessed is your true name.
We pray for your reign of peace to come,
We pray that your good will be done,
Let heaven and earth become one.
Give us this day the bread we need,
Give it to those who have none.
Let forgiveness flow like a river between us,
From each one to each one.
Lead us to holy innocence
Beyond the evil of our days —
Come swiftly Mother, Father, come.
For yours is the power and the glory
and the mercy:
Forever your name is All in One.

   — Parker Palmer

Collect

Almighty and eternal God,
so draw our hearts to you,
so guide our minds,
so fill our imaginations,
so control our wills,
that we may be wholly yours,
utterly dedicated to you;
and then use us, we pray, as you will,
and always to your glory and the welfare of your people;
through our Lord and Savior Jesus Christ.
Amen.

   —"A Prayer of Self-Dedication," The Book of Common Prayer, p. 832

Sharing

THE CATHEDRAL OF THE INCARNATION in Baltimore has a large baptismal font that sits prominently in the crossing, just in front of the altar. I remember being surprised by the font the first time I walked into the sanctuary. I was in Maryland interviewing for the position I now hold as Missioner for Christian Education and Formation, and I decided to visit the cathedral in order to pray and try to sense if this was the place I might belong. I entered by a side door, sat in the second pew, and began to meditate. After a few moments, I looked up, and there, in front of me, was the font. I got up and went closer. There was water in the basin! And strewn along the bottom, under the clear glass bowl that lined the font, was a lovely display of pressed fresh flowers. I placed my hand in the water and began to pray. I felt a great assurance from that water—poured into that beautifully decorated basin which stood right at the front of the nave. I had long longed for such a liturgical space, one that spoke of baptism as central, but I had never seen it. Before I left the cathedral that day, I had decided to take the risk of moving to this new job, in this new place.

Now, whenever I can, I worship at the cathedral. As we approach the Lord's table for Communion, all stop and touch the water. Children beg to be lifted up to see and touch it, too. I have come to learn that the font was placed in this spot, right in front of the altar, about ten years ago, as an outward and visible sign of the cathedral's coming to see itself as a baptismal and eucharistic community. It had not always been so.

The congregation had been slowly dying. Few worshiped there. The bishop considered disbanding the congregation. Instead, a new dean was called to rebuild the church. The community and new dean prayed and wrestled with whom they were called to be in that place. The Spirit led them to the water and to the vows made at baptism, and it fed them at the table. Worship, especially baptism, became central. In response, they changed their liturgical space to reflect who they were becoming. It was not long before the congregation's focus turned outward. They joined the urban "Harbor Region" grouping of Episcopal churches. The vestry decided they needed a better knowledge of the city. Consequently, they planned a vestry weekend "retreat" at the downtown YMCA that required them to fan out over the community to experience a variety of Baltimore realities—some riding shifts with police officers, some working in shelters, others visiting a prison. They reconvened at the YMCA to reflect on what they had learned and what their new awareness meant for the mission of their church. One result was that the parish joined the Habitat for Humanity group in Sandtown, a desolate neighborhood near the cathedral. They have since built a dozen houses there, helping turn the neighborhood around. Every Palm Sunday, congregation members make a "Peace Walk" from their current Habitat project to the cathedral, stopping at other outreach projects along the way, to pray for peace and justice in the city.

One Sunday in early 1997, someone brought in a newspaper clipping. It told of a child, James Smith III, who was fatally shot on his third birthday. The boy's mother had taken him for a special haircut before his birthday celebration. He was killed in the crossfire of two nineteen-year-olds.

"Will you persevere in resisting evil?...Will you seek and serve Christ in all persons?... Will you strive for justice and peace?...Will you love... respect dignity... resist evil...?" The cathedral could no longer tolerate what was happening so near them. They prayed for guidance in their corporate response, and marked their concern ritually. On the Sunday following the fatal shooting, they placed a votive candle on the altar, and remembered James in the Prayers of the People. Ever since, on any Sunday following the

violent death of a Baltimore child, a votive candle is lit on the altar. The congregation prays for the child and, at the Peace, an acolyte processes the candle to a small nook in the back of the sanctuary that is filled with other lighted candles serving as a memorial to children lost to violence. The candle remains there with the others, all of them burning brightly at every service of worship. A banner hangs alongside the candles, bearing the names of the all the lost children; and there is a scrapbook that contains their obituaries and newspaper reports of the violence that took them. Annually, on Holy Innocents' Day, all the children killed the previous year are remembered in a liturgy in which cathedral children process from the children's memorial, bearing the commemorative candles forward and placing them around the font.

As cathedral prayers shifted to include needs of the city—particularly those of children—so did cathedral ministries. Members became active in a Baltimore group called "Advocates for Children and Youth," and the congregation "adopted" their local district school, serving the students in any number of ways as needs arose. On election day, members of the congregation break out cathedral lapel pins that bear the slogan, "Children can't vote; I vote for them." They have explored how to provide "safe space" for city children and, as a result, now host a "Children's Peace Center" one Saturday a month. Plans are underway to expand to weekly events, and even to export some version of the program to other city churches.

The Cathedral of the Incarnation heeded a call to urban ministry and advocacy for children. Because of it, the congregation has never been the same. Sunday mornings, a diverse group gathers for worship, with every manner and persuasion of folk filling the sanctuary to capacity. For several years they have had a Thursday evening Taizé Eucharist for peace and reconciliation. Recently they added a quiet Sunday evening service of Compline and Eucharist. It too is focused on peace, with readings taken from scripture and other sources. Spanish and Igbo congregations also now meet there regularly. The Cathedral has grown in numbers, and in grace. It is now not only *not* dying, but the living water of baptism is flowing from the congregation into the city.

AFTER BOTH MY PARENTS died, no family lived in Maine anymore, which meant taking care of our summer place on Sand Pond was difficult. At the same time, I found myself tired, discouraged, frustrated with church life, and no longer sure of God, let alone my call. So, in 2006, I decided to go home to Maine. No job, no plan. I just had to leave the work of nearly twenty years and return to the place where I felt most rooted.

In exploring where to live, Lewiston became an option. It was only a forty-minute drive from the lake so it was familiar from grocery shopping each summer, and sometimes I attended church there as the priest at the time was a friend. I knew that if I was ever to go to church again, I would need a community that was making a difference and Trinity was, deeply committed to its impoverished neighborhood. I also knew that I would likely not attend church any more if I had to drive any distance to get there. All that made Lewiston worth a look.

A friend, Marguerite, who lived across the river in Auburn, offered to drive me around one day to show me more of the town. At one point she drove into the parking lot of something called Wisdom's Center and told me about the nuns who had opened it a few years back as a center for women and their children. It was late in the day and they were closed, but one of the nuns, who I now know was Sister Irene, came out the door and spoke with us briefly through the car window.

Upon leaving the parking lot, I turned to Marguerite and proclaimed "Well, I guess I am moving to Lewiston! I think my future is tied up here!" The decision was made, in a flash.

The following summer soon after arriving, I started volunteering at Wisdom's Center. I thought I was going there to help, when in fact it was me who needed healing. The four nuns tended to me gently. What I found in them helped rebuild my faith and life. They are Daughters of Wisdom, and as I learned who they were, I was amazed.

Founded in France over three centuries ago, their spirituality is that of seeking Wisdom in ordinary, everyday experience, and they believe that all reality, all creation and all humankind, all joys and struggles, are interconnected and sacred. They seek and contemplate Divine Wisdom present in a world that hungers for meaning, justice and compassion. For them, that Divine Wisdom is the feminine face of God—Sophia. Jesus is Wisdom incarnate, present to anyone experiencing injustice, violence, poverty and oppression. That charism, in practice over centuries, has been focused on women and children.

I had read and studied feminist theology. I had attended an all-girl high school, and for years went to a retreat center in Maine called Greenfire, that was for women only. Why had I never heard of these sisters?

Slowly over the next few years, as I watched them tend to the most marginalized women with immense patience, care, and concern, they mentored me. Their love restored my soul and opened my heart. I became an Associate of Wisdom. Eventually, their work became mine, so much so that when they needed to let the work go, Trinity Church and I carried it on.

The center, now "The Center for Wisdom's Women," has grown, and in 2019 "Sophia's House" was opened in a former convent, just down the street. It is a residential community of healing for women that includes those who have experienced trafficking/exploitation, incarceration, and addiction. In retiring, I now live there as one of the tenants, as mentor and ally to others.

Now, fifteen years later, looking back, there is no way anyone could have guessed the path that opened. And the God of my understanding is now more fluid and relational and real than I could have ever imagined.

For Small Group Discussion

Reach into the bowl of water and take one of the river rocks. Hold it. Feel how smooth it is. Years of being washed by fast-moving water have rounded the rough edges.

What rough edges have been smoothed in your life?

What has come back to life in you, after having been dead?

What river are you following?

Who is with you on the journey?

Tell a story about a time when you were remarkably aware of the abundance of God's grace and love.

Tell a story about a time when you knew you were following a call, and saw things change because of it.

Reflecting

Scripture

Exodus 17:1–6	Water from a rock
1 Samuel 3	The call of Samuel
Psalm 46	Be still and know that I am God
Psalm 57:7–10	My heart is steadfast
Ezekiel 37:1–14	Valley of the dry bones
Joel 2:23–29	God's spirit pours out
Isaiah 6:6–8	Here I am; send me
Isaiah 43:18–21	I am about to do a new thing
Matthew 7:24–27 *(Luke 6:47–49)*	House built on rock and sand
Matthew 22:34–40	Love the Lord your God
John 4:7–15	Samaritan Woman
Romans 12:1–2	Be transformed
2 Corinthians 5:17–21	New creation
Ephesians 3:14–21	A prayer of Paul
Revelation 7:13–17	Springs of life
Revelation 21:1–7	Vision of a new heaven and new earth
Revelation 22:1–5	River of life

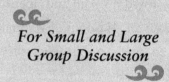

For Small and Large Group Discussion

Refer to the scripture selections. Choose one or two that speak to you and discuss them.

What word or phrase jumps out at you?

What does the passage say to you?

What is it calling you to do?

Consider any of the suggested hymns that relate to your conversation. Read over the Prayer Book selections and comments.

What light do they shed on your conversation?

Hymns

The Hymnal 1982

> Lord of all hopefulness, #482
> Be thou my vision, #488
> Breathe on me, Breath of God, #508
> Glorious things of thee are spoken, #522
> Jesus calls us; o'er the tumult, #549
> God be in my head, and in my understanding, #694
> Take my life, and let it be, #707

Wonder, Love, and Praise

> The desert shall rejoice and blossom, #722
> Will you come and follow me, #757
> Thuma mina, #808
> I, the Lord of sea and sky, #812
> Guide my feet Lord, #819

Lift Every Voice and Sing II

> Deep river, #8
> Here I am, send me, #126
> I have decided to follow Jesus, #136
> Shall we gather at the river, #141

The Book of Common Prayer

Collects, The Season after Pentecost, pp. 228–236
"For All Baptized Christians," Collects for Various Occasions, p. 252
"For all Christians in their vocations," Collect III,
> For the Ministry (Ember Days), p. 256
Collect for purity, p. 323 (Rite I), p. 355 (Rite II)
Postcommunion Prayer, pp. 365–366
"For those about to be Baptized or renew their Baptismal Covenant,"
> Prayers for the Church, p. 819
The Catechism:
> The Church, pp. 854–855
> The Ministry, pp. 855–856

The Catechism tells us that a sacrament is an "outward and visible sign of an inward and spiritual grace." Baptism is the sacrament by which God adopts us, making us part of Christ's Body, the Church, and inheritors of the kingdom of God. The outward and visible sign is the water in which we are baptized. The inward and spiritual graces are many: union with Christ; birth in God's family, the Church; forgiveness of sins; and new life in the Holy Spirit.

Baptism certainly marks a change in us, but it does not end there. We don't emerge from the water fully formed, with it all put together. It wasn't even that way for Jesus. His struggles continued long after he left the Jordan River. Our experience of baptism is a change of heart that must become a way of life. The conversion of heart may begin when we are baptized, but the process is not over until we die. In between, we are opened to God and to others, bit by bit. The river flowing through us smoothes the stones, and carves away layers of sediment. It is process of constant cleansing, until we reach a point where the water of life flows through us, and out of us, bringing life to the desert of others' lives. When that happens, it is another outward and visible sign of our having been baptized. Your kingdom come, O God, your will be done, right here on earth, as it is in heaven.

❖　　❖　　❖

For Small or Large Group Discussion

Turn to the section of the Prayer Book Catechism called "The Church" and read the three questions at the very top of page 855 that relate to the church's mission.

In what ways does your congregation carry out the mission of the church?

How might it do a better job?

Where in your community and in the world do you see a lack of unity with God?

What would it take to restore unity?

In the section of the Prayer Book Catechism called "The Ministry" (also on page 855), read the answer to the question, "What is the ministry of the laity?"

What is your ministry in daily life?

How has your ministry developed?

What events in your life have led you to the place you are now?

Do you ever sense God directing you? If so, how? Do you resist listening?

What has kept you from seeking or following God's guidance?

When in your life were you sure you were doing God's will? How did you know it?

In the Lord's Prayer, we pray, "your kingdom come, your will be done, on earth as in heaven." Jesus told us that the kingdom of God was among us.

In what ways have you experienced God's kingdom among us?

If God's kingdom fully reigned on earth, what would change?

How do/might you participate in God's mission of bringing in the kingdom?

The Dean of the Cathedral of the Incarnation stays a few weeks each summer at our lake cottage in Maine. He is an avid fly fisherman. He goes to the Kennebec River every afternoon to fish, returning much past dark. He never keeps what he catches. "It is not the fish," he says, "but the fishing that is important."

Not long ago, the Kennebec, like many rivers in Maine, was a dying river. Too much pollution from the paper industry, along with sewage and who-knows-what-else, had been dumped in the water over the years. I am told that, sometimes, it smelled. There were few fish in the river in those days, and those that remained were not fit to eat.

One day late last summer, with great glee, the Dean told me about standing in the middle of the river at sunset the previous evening, when the water was so alive with trout that he was sure one of them would jump into his boot! What a change! The once dying river is now teeming with life!

O Sapiencia

O Sapientia, quae ex ore Altissimi prodiisti,
attingens a fine usque ad finem,
fortiter suaviterque disponens omnia:
veni ad docendum nos viam prudentiae.

O Wisdom, proceeding from the mouth of the Most High,
pervading and permeating the whole creation,
mightily ordering all things:
Come and teach us the way of prudence.

— The first of the O Antiphons in Advent.

O Come, O Come Emmanuel

O Come, O Come thou Wisdom from on high,
Who orderest all things mightily:
To us the path of knowledge show,
And teach us in her ways to go.
Rejoice! Rejoice! Emmanuel
Shall come to thee, O Israel.

— Hymnal 1982 #56

Breathe on me Breath of God,
fill me with life a-new,
that I may love what thou dost love,
and do what thou wouldst do.

Breathe on me Breath of God,
until my heart is pure,
until with thee I will one will,
to do or to endure.

Breathe of me Breath of God,
till I am wholly thine,
till all this earthly part of me
glows with the fire divine.

Breathe on me Breath of God,
so shall I never die;
but live with thee the perfect life
of thine eternity.

— The Hymnal 1982 #508, words by
Edwin Hatch. A lovely setting of this is
recorded by The Miserable Offenders
on their CD "God Help Us."

Grand Canyon

They say the layered earth rose up
Ancient rock leviathan
Trailing ages in its wake
Lifting earthmass toward the sun
And coursing water cut the rock away
To leave these many-storied walls
Exposé of ages gone
Around this breathless emptiness
More wondrous far than earth had ever known

My life has risen layered too
Each day, each year in turn has left
Its fossil life and sediments
Evidence of lived and unlived hours
The tedium, the anguish, yes the joy
That some heart-deep vitality
Keeps pressing upward toward the day I die

And Spirit cuts like water through it all
Carving out this emptiness
So inner eye can see
The soaring height of canyon walls within
Walls whose very color, texture, form
Redeem in beauty all my life has been
The darkness and the light, the false, the true
While deep below the living waters run
Cutting deeper through my parts
To resurrect my gravebound heart

Making, always making, all things new
— Parker J. Palmer, *The Weavings Reader*, ed. John Mogabgab

Every birth is a new creation;
every greeting a prayer;
every washing a baptism;
every meal a Eucharist;
every sleeping and waking
a dying and rising in Christ –
because each person is the
one for whom Christ died.
— W. Paul Jones, *A Table in the Desert: Making Space Holy*

Let us remain
as empty
as possible
so that God
can fill us up.
— Mother Teresa

My Lord God, I have no idea where I am going. I do not see the road ahead of me. I cannot know for certain where it will end. Nor do I really know myself, and the fact that I think that I am following your will does not mean that I am actually doing so. But I believe that the desire to please you does in fact please you. And I hope I have that desire in all that I am doing. I hope that I will never do anything apart from that desire. And I know that if I do this you will lead me by the right road, though I may know nothing about it. Therefore will I trust you always, though I may seem to be lost and in the shadow of death. I will not fear, for you are ever with me, and you will never leave me to face my perils alone.

— Thomas Merton

Have patience with everything unresolved in your heart and try to love the questions themselves ... the point is, to live everything. Live the questions now. Perhaps then, you will gradually, without even noticing it, live your way into the answer.

— Rainer Maria Rilke, *Letters to a Young Poet*, second letter

Let yourself be plumbed to the depths, and you will realize that everyone is created for a presence. There, in your heart of hearts, in that place where no two people are alike, Christ is waiting for you. And there the unexpected happens.

— Brother Roger of Taizé, *A Life We Never Dared Hope For*, p. 77

Crashing Water at Creation

Crashing water at creation
    ordered by the Spirit's breath,
first to witness day's beginning
    from the brightness of night's death.

Parting water stood and trembled
    as the captives passed on through,
washing off the chains of bondage—
    channel to a life made new.

Cleansing water once at Jordan
    closed around the One foretold,
Opened to reveal the glory
    ever new and ever old.

Living water, never ending,
    quench the thirst and flood the soul.
Wellspring, Source of life eternal,
    drench our dryness, make us whole.

        — Sylvia Dunstan,
        The New Century Hymnal, #326

Do not draw consolation only from the scriptures written in ink, for God's grace also writes the laws of the Spirit directly on the tablet of the heart.

        —Pseudo-Macarius,
        4th century monk

"The place God calls you to is the place where your deep gladness and the world's deep hunger meet."

        — Frederich Buechner, *Wishful Thinking: A Theological ABC*, p. 95

The many-voiced song of the river echoed softly. Siddhartha looked into the river and saw many pictures in the flowing water. The river's voice was sorrowful. It sang with yearning and sadness, flowing towards its goal ... Siddhartha ... was now listening intently ... to this song of a thousand voices...then the great song of a thousand voices consisted of one word: Om—perfection.... From that hour Siddhartha ceased to fight against his destiny.

        — Hermann Hesse, *Siddhartha*

My Life Flows on in Endless Song

My life flows on in endless song;
    above heart's lamentation,
I hear the sweet, though far-off hymn
    that hails a new creation.
Through all the tumult and the strife,
    I hear the music ringing;
It finds an echo in my soul—
    how can I keep from singing?

What though my joys and comforts die?
    My Savior still is living.
What thought the shadows gather 'round?
    A new song Christ is giving.
No storm can shake my inmost calm,
    while to that Rock I'm clinging;
Since Love commands both heaven and earth,
    how can I keep from singing?

When tyrants tremble, sick with fear,
    and hear their death knells ringing;
When friends rejoice both far and near,
    how can I keep from singing?
In prison cell and dungeon vile
    our thoughts to them are winging;
When friends by shame are undefiled,
    how can I keep from singing?

I lift my eyes; the cloud grows thin;
    I see the blue above it;
And day by day this pathway smoothes,
    since first I learned to love it.
The peace of Christ makes fresh my heart,
    a fountain ever springing;
All things are mine since I am Christ's
    how can I keep from singing?

— anonymous, as found in
Bright Jewels for the Sunday School,
ed. Robert Lowery, 1869

永

With the word for "eternity," we come full circle. In Session One, we were given the Chinese character for "water," which evolved from a symbol showing the main flow of a river with eddies swirling from the sides. The Chinese word for eternity has the same strokes with the addition of a spot of ink above the main flow of the river, representing a complex concept of "foreverness" as a flow that never ends.

Christ has no body but yours,
No hands, no feet on earth but yours,
Yours are the eyes with which He looks
Compassion on this world,
Yours are the feet with which He
    walks to do good,
Yours are the hands, with which He
    blesses all the world.
Yours are the hands, yours are the feet,
Yours are the eyes, you are His body.
Christ has no body now but yours,
No hands, no feet on earth but yours,
Yours are the eyes with which he looks
compassion on this world.
Christ has no body now on earth but yours.

— St. Teresa of Ávila (attributed)

Breathe on me Breath of God

Breathe on me Breath of God,
fill me with life a-new,
that I may love what thou dost love,
and do what thou wouldst do.

Breathe on me Breath of God,
until my heart is pure,
until with thee I will one will,
to do or to endure.

Breathe of me Breath of God,
till I am wholly thine,
till all this earthly part of me
glows with the fire divine.

Breathe on me Breath of God,
so shall I never die;
but live with thee the perfect life
of thine eternity.

— The Hymnal 1982 #508, words by Edwin
Hatch. A lovely setting of this is recorded by
The Miserable Offenders on their CD "God
Help Us" available from Morehouse Barlow.

There is a God-shaped vacuum in the human heart which
only God, made known through Jesus Christ, can fill.

— a thought often attributed to Pascal

Holy and Creative Spirit

Holy and creative Spirit,
    source of primal birth:
Out of uncorrupted waters
    you brought forth earth;
As crown of your creation,
    you breathed all flesh to life.
Stir up our will to keep your world
    from wanton waste and strife.

Holy and redemptive Spirit,
    liberating power
When your children were in bondage
    in their darkest hour;
You guided and released them
    beyond the parted sea.
Break now the chains that fetter us;
    set every people free.

Holy and anointing Spirit,
    calling some apart:
After Jesus rose from Jordan
    you enflamed his heart;
You sent him forth with Good News
    for those with many needs.
Raise up today a servant church
    to follow where he leads.

Holy and renewing Spirit,
    working in us still:
Through Baptism's cleansing water
    you forgave self-will;
You raise us to a new life
    with the eternal Son.
Help us affirm the victory
    which Jesus Christ has won.

Holy and embracing Spirit,
    Reaching out for all:
In your ceaseless, surging rhythms
    We have heard your call;
You fill us with your music
    And send us forth to sing
To humankind throughout the earth
    That Christ is Lord and King.

— A. Theodore Eastman, 1975 (unpublished)

May God bless you and keep you.
May God turn God's face toward you,
    and be gracious to you;
May God lift up God's countenance
    upon you, and give you peace.

— Numbers 6:24-26 (adapted)

May the road rise to meet you. May the wind be always at your back. And may God hold you in the hollow of God's hand.

— Irish blessing

Responding

Practicing Together:

- As this final session comes to a close, share stories about your spiritual journey and celebrate them with song. Give everyone a chance to think of an experience in the last month when they felt God present in their lives, or a recent time when they clearly lived one of their baptismal vows.

  Invite one person to briefly tell the story that has come to mind.

  Sing a hymn that echoes the person's story in some way. Anyone in the group can suggest a hymn. It may be one of the hymns used in one of the sessions.

  Repeat this process, with another person sharing a story, and then the group responding with a hymn.

  When everyone who wishes to do so has shared a story, invite all participants to comment on any common themes they hear in the stories.

  Close with the prayers suggested at the end of the session.
  — adapted from "Authority of All Generations," a process created by Ernesto Medina

- Spend some time looking at the entries in *Lesser Feasts and Fasts*. Ask participants to name a favorite saint. Look up that saint and read the biography. If your church has a patron saint, read that biography. Read the stories of saints appointed for days nearest the date on which you do this exercise. Talk about what you learn from their life stories. Invite each person to create a similar entry (life story, scripture passage, and collect) for someone they know and admire. Share the stories.

- Read about how the early church celebrated baptism. One particular essay by Aidan Kavanagh is "A Rite of Passage," which can be found in the appendix. Another beautiful story called "Sonia's Baptism" from El Salvador can be found in the book *Gifts of Many Cultures*, pp. 110-111. Describe a recent baptism you have witnessed, or if you know it, share the story of your own baptism. In what ways do they differ?

- Pair up the individuals in the group and invite each person to write a blessing for the other. See the classic blessings on the previous page. These will be read during the closing prayer.

Practicing at Home:

- Make a graph of your spiritual journey. Draw a straight line across the middle of a piece of paper turned lengthwise. Divide this center line into even blocks of years. Then, in relation to this center line, draw another winding line that represents your life, as follows: for those times in your life that you felt close to God, draw a "hill" above the center line; for those times that you felt at a distance to God, draw a "valley" below the center line; on the "hills" and "valleys," make notations about what was happening in your life at that time.

- Periodically, as an examination of your life and ministry, take time to pray the Baptismal Covenant. Use the prayer sheet in the appendix, "Praying the Baptismal Covenant."

- Learn the hymn, "Breathe on me, Breath of God," in *The Hymnal 1982*, #508. Sing or speak the words as a prayer each morning. There is a wonderful setting of this hymn on the recording *God Help Us* by the Miserable Offenders. Another prayerful hymn that is good for evening is "Be Thou My Vision," *The Hymnal 1982*, #488.

Closing Prayer

Sing again the Opening Song, "Peace is flowing like a river," which was sung in the time of Gathering.

Take a moment to share thanksgivings and personal prayer needs.

Close with the following prayer and blessing.

O Holy Spirit, giver of all life through the water of creation and the womb of the cross:
Guide us as we seek to give birth to you in our lives and in the world around us;
in the name of God, our Mother, our Wisdom, and our Comforter. Amen.

— Elizabeth Rankin Geitz, *Women's Uncommon Prayers*, p. 317

If the group did the exercise in Practicing Together, to write a blessing for another member of the group, have each person read the blessing they wrote for their partner. You may wish to have a small bottle of oil on hand and have them make the sign of the cross on each other's palms after reading the blessings.

Give each person a bunch of greenery, and have them dip it in the water. Then sprinkle each other. Have fun with this. Use lots of water. Proclaim: "Remember your baptism, and be thankful!"

Sing or speak the "Sprinkling Song" from the Reflecting section.
Close with the following prayer:

Almighty God, we thank you that by the death and resurrection of your Son Jesus Christ you have overcome sin and brought us to yourself, and that by the sealing of your Holy Spirit you have bound us to your service. Renew in us the covenant you made with us at our Baptism. Send us forth in the power of that Spirit to perform the service you set before us; through Jesus Christ your Son our Lord, who lives and reigns with you and the Holy Spirit, one God, now and for ever. Amen.

— The Book of Common Prayer, p. 309 (adapted)

Epilogue

**"Will you cherish the wondrous works of God,
and protect the beauty and integrity of all creation?"**

(A new baptismal covenant vow authorized for trial use at General Convention 2015, and fully authorized in 2018)

The following contributions come from folks at Trinity Church, Lewiston, Maine, and are seeds for a new chapter of Living Water. It is up to you to expand the chapter, and if you choose to, you may share your stories and resources on the Living Water web page (http://www. livingwaterbaptism.net). On that page you can also share additional material for the original vows or ask for suggestions and offer ideas for how you live the waters of baptism in daily life.

Gathering

Collect a variety of leaves, berries, stones, flowers, pine cones and other natural objects and lay them around the bowl of water. Get a copy of the 1998 edition of Rachel Carson's 1956 classic The Book of Wonder, *and lay it open, in view.*

OPENING SONG: **The Land We're Walking On**

This land we're walking on, it all belongs to You 2x
Alleluia, alleluia, and let us walk with You 2x

Give us the forgiveness, and let us walk with You 2x
Alleluia, alleluia, and let us walk with You 2x

Let the gate of heaven open, and let us walk in with You 2x
Alleluia, alleluia, and let us walk with You 2x

This chant is by a 20th-century fiddler from Newfoundland, Emile Benoit, 1913-1992.
It was recorded in the last year of his life in the company of a younger generation putting their spin on his music. I find this chant very moving in its simple and beautiful melody and in the barebones text, each verse a moving progression from its previous. And, it's the best minor key alleluia since Leonard Cohen! *– Greg Boardman*
You can listen to the recording here: https://www.youtube.com/watch?v=k1etut1-3gc

SCRIPTURE
John 1:1-18
Psalm 148 (from St. Helena Breviary, p. 541),
 or Benedicite (St. Helena Breviary, p. 120),
 or one of the canticles for Rogation Days (St. Helena Breviary, pp. 257, 259)

Sharing

MAINE AUDUBON HAS a program called "Bringing Nature Home" based on a book of the same name by Douglas Tallamy. It talks about how anyone can sustain wildlife with native plants. They have been encouraging people to change their landscaping habits. The project has taken root more in suburban and rural areas. This kind of landscaping is suited to the local climate and soil, it attracts native insects and then attract and feed the native birds, and pollinators evolved locally to eat native plants. Cultivars just don't provide the right nourishment.

Sophia's House where I live, and Trinity Church two blocks away, have both partnered with Maine Audubon as demonstration projects to show that even in a dense urban environment we can, and should, do this.

For two summers, the residents of Sophia's House have been landscaping their property by planting hundreds of plugs of a sedge for a lawn, instead of grass. There are two beach plum bushes, one hazelnut, two service berry trees, three spice bushes, swamp milkweed, a native arborvitae and several native groundcovers. A row of blueberry seedlings will become an edible hedge along the sidewalk. We also put in several small raised beds for a kitchen garden of herbs and small vegetables.

At the church, in our small memorial garden, we first had to eradicate an invasive goutweed plant that had taken over. It took twice cutting it back to the ground followed by two treatments of herbicide. Next summer we will be planting in its place all sorts of wild flowers such as penstemon and columbine for spring blooms, black-eyed susan and purple coneflowers for mid-summer, swamp and butterfly milkweed as forage for hungry monarch caterpillars in late July and August, Liatris and three kinds of native asters to support butterflies and other pollinators as well as migrating birds in the fall. We have winter sown the seeds of these plants, which came from the Maine Wild Seed Project, in milk jugs to live outside all winter. Hopefully they will sprout in the spring! As at Sophia's House, native sedge will fill in the open spots along with some wild ginger and foamflowers.

Then we will wait eagerly for butterflies, bees, and birds to show up and feast on the foods that they are meant to consume. A sign on the church fence explains what we are doing and invites people to help. More educational signage will be added as we go along, in both locations. We also plan to post a land acknowledgment in the garden.

Already, as we work in the two yards and people walk by, they stop and ask what we are doing. It is becoming a powerful way to engage our neighbors and bring new life into our concrete and asphalt surroundings. Our hope is to inspire, encourage and teach others to do the same.

Seeing the Future
– by Jane Costlow

ON A SUNNY DAY in July, I walk with a happy assortment of ten- and eleven-year old kids from the Tree Street center to a park along the river. A woman named Julie from the National Park Service has already arrived with a truckload of fishing gear. Along with volunteers from a local land trust we're going to teach these inner-city kids to fish. Just because they're growing up in crowded walk-up apartment buildings doesn't mean they don't have every child's curiosity about the outdoors. There are little girls in colorful hijabs, boys who are confident they already "know how to fish" because they've been with an uncle. There are kids who are shy about the whole process, and then discover the delight of tossing a weighted line (without hook) in the air. For a brief moment the open meadow above the river is filled with laughter and the more-or-less organized chaos of bright filaments whooshing through the air.

The English folk who founded Trinity Church came to design mills that would drive the development of this community. They came from Manchester and Liverpool, places where English industrialists had already built the "dark satanic mills" that William Blake wrote about. The dream for Lewiston, like other New England mill towns, was that industry and nature could co-exist. The city park—now Kennedy Park—was meant to be a place of pure air and refreshment; the mills themselves were set among canals that drew river water into a great labyrinth of flywheels and belts to power machinery.

The painter Marsden Hartley, who as a boy sang in the Trinity choir, remembered the mills as "monstrous, terrifying prison-like…" They employed thousands of men and women, many of them French Catholics who came south from Quebec. They spun bedspreads and garments from wool and cotton: cotton that before the Civil War had been picked by enslaved people in the south; wool that came from the vast numbers of sheep turned out to graze on Maine's deforested late-19th century hillsides. By the mid-twentieth century the Androscoggin River was one of the ten most polluted rivers in the country.

Cotton dust and bleaching chemicals—along with the refuse of upstream paper mills and untreated sewage—spilled into the river and clogged workers' lungs. Instead of salmon and alewives and eels the river was filled with huge pillows of foam that collected during the summer when the water was low.

Almost fifty years later—after Maine Senator's Edmund Muskie managed to pass the Clean Water Act—the Androscoggin has been transformed. There are eels and bass—though not yet salmon or alewives in anything like the abundance there once were. The air doesn't make you want to wretch, and the cotton particles that workers breathed in the hot, humid air of the mills are gone. On summer days you can see people kayaking, or fishing, or simply sitting by the water enjoying the play of light. But we still live in the shadow of the great mills—mostly empty now—and the city is marked by the kinds of poverty and slow erosion of the environment that linger in hollowed-out, post-industrial communities.

In Lewiston—and at Trinity—we inhabit both past and present, and try to imagine—and create—a healthier future. For ourselves, for these children, for the alewives and salmon. Communities like this keep us honest—they keep us close to concrete realities of poverty and struggle and environmental degradation. But they also give us opportunities every day to "practice resurrection," as Wendell Berry puts it.

When I watch kids learning to fish in a park that used to be an industrial waste site, I can almost see that future rising before me.

2021 Annual Loon Count Shows Importance of Long Term Studies
— by Maine Audubon Staff   November 28, 2021   https://maineaudubon.org

ADULTS UP, CHICKS DOWN, but what does it all mean? As Maine Audubon releases the data from its 2021 Annual Loon Count, it underscores the importance of long-term studies and highlights the need to look beyond the one-day count to understand the data.

The annual loon count takes place on the third Saturday of July, and for the 2021 count, more than 1400 volunteers jumped into their skiffs, boats, and kayaks on a mostly clear, calm day throughout the state, with early morning fog obscuring viewing on just a small number of lakes. Approximately fifty loon counters who weren't able to make the count last year due to COVID-19-related reasons once again joined the count, so volunteers were able to look for loons on 328 lakes, 20 more than in 2020.

The result: Estimates for the adult population are up, from 2974 last year to 3446 this year. These estimates are for areas south of the 45th parallel—roughly south of a line from Rangeley to Calais—where enough lakes are counted in order to make a reliable estimate.

Loon Count Manager Tracy Hart says, "We had been watching a two-year decline in the adult population that began in 2019 and showed a further reduction in 2020. We are happy to report that adult numbers are back up this year and estimated to be even higher than ever, continuing the general upward trend and recovery that we have seen throughout the history of the loon count."

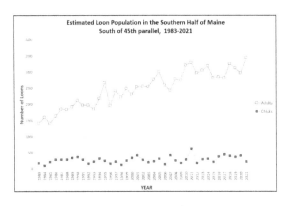

However, chick estimates were down from 414 last year to 224 this year. Hart says it's too early to tell if that marks a temporary dip or a new trend for loon chicks, but that similar and even more pronounced dips have been noticed multiple times in the 38 years of the Maine Audubon loon count and the chick population has rebounded each time. She says, "We aren't certain why chick numbers are down this season, but it is likely a combination of reduced nesting success from early extreme rainstorms which flooded some nests; washouts from boat wakes; aggression from non-nesting loons; chick or egg predation; some nests being abandoned due to human disturbance, and chicks being run over by boats. In addition, sometimes loons simply take a break from nesting—they don't necessarily breed or breed successfully every year."

The Annual Loon Count provides a vital snapshot of the population at the same time and with the same methods each year. It is like a barometer that shows biologists how the population is doing compared to prior years and helps track those changes over time. But there's still much more to learn about Maine's loon population. That's why Hart is particularly excited about the expansion of loon conservation and outreach programs, thanks to new funding sources. Earlier this year, Maine Audubon received a five-year grant to significantly expand the Maine Loon Project, and to partner with Maine Lakes, Lakes Environmental Association, and the Penobscot Indian Nation to work to improve loon productivity and reduce mortality in the state. The new partnership is an exciting opportunity to work with local volunteers to start documenting loon successes and failures in more depth. It will be a complement to the Annual Loon Count, with the count still serving as the cornerstone in tracking the population, and this new effort providing additional avenues to understand and address the issues on individual lakes and ponds.

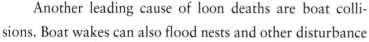

Since the loon count's inception, the number of adult loons in the southern half of the state has essentially doubled, from an initial estimate of fewer than 1,500 to nearly 3,000 in 2020. The growth is thanks to conservation efforts like the Maine lead tackle ban and the Fish Lead Free Initiative that helped reduce the number of adult loons dying from swallowing lead tackle.

Another leading cause of loon deaths are boat collisions. Boat wakes can also flood nests and other disturbance can cause loons to abandon their nests. Tracy Hart says, "We encourage people to slow down, especially near islands and lakeshores, stay away from loon families, and learn to read the signs that loons use to tell you that you're just too close." For more information see the brochure "Living in Loon Territory," available on the Maine Audubon website. A possible new threat is predation from the successful rise in the population of eagles.

I have learned that loons do not mate until several years old, and return to their birth pond until they do mate. Generally, there is one mating pair per smaller pond. Larger ponds may have more than one mating pair. Loons continue to be a fragile species and every year we wait for the loon count results.

The results of the 2021 count are not yet fully available, but last year in our pond, Sand Pond, Tacoma Lakes, the count was 8 adults, but no chicks. In the adjoining four other ponds of Tacoma Lakes that year, there was a total of 31 adults, 6 chicks. This summer while out in the kayak, I did see an adult pair with two chicks on our pond! One day late summer I saw a loon party of 9 adults gathered. Seeing them and listening to them is one of the joys of the summers.

The last years have brought a new threat to the ponds, Eurasian Milfoil and other non-native invasive water species. They are plants that can quickly and literally choke a lake to death. It is near impossible and very expensive to eradicate. A few surrounding lakes have been infested, but so far, not Tacoma Lakes.

This summer I finally joined the invasive plant patrol that goes out weekly in kayaks to scope the lake shore waters for signs of infestations. Other volunteers staff the boat launch to inspect boats for bits of unwanted plants before they put in. It would take only one small fragment to infect the clear waters forever.

Reflecting

Passages appointed for Rogation Days

Deuteronomy 11:10-15
Psalm 147
Romans 8:18-25
Mark 4:26-32

Ecclesiasticus 38:27-32
Psalm 107:1-9
I Corinthians 3:10-14
Matthew 6:19-24

For Hildegard of Bingen

Ecclesiasticus 43:1–12
Psalm 104:25–34
John 3:16-21

Hildegard of Bingen (1098-1179)

"The earth is at the same time mother,
she is mother of all that is natural,
mother of all that is human.
She is the mother of all,
for contained in her are the seeds of all.
The earth of humankind contains all moisture,
all verdancy, all germinating power.
It is in so many ways fruitful.
All creation comes from it.
Yet it forms not only the basic raw materials
for humankind, but also
the substance of Incarnation."

"For the beauty of the Earth"

For the beauty of the earth
For the beauty of the skies
For the love which from our birth
Over and around us lies.

Refrain: Christ our God, to thee we raise
this our hymn of grateful praise.

For the beauty of each hour
Of the day and of the night
Hill and vale, and tree and flower,
Sun and moon and stars of light.

— *The Hymnal 1982*, #416
Words: Folliot Sanford Pierpoint

"Glance at the sun. See the moon and the stars.
Gaze at the beauty of the Earth's greenings. Now, think."
— Hildegard of Bingen

"A child's world is fresh and new and beautiful, full of wonder and excitement. It is our misfortune that for most of us that clear-eyed vision, that true instinct for what is beautiful and awe-inspiring, is diminished and even lost before we reach adulthood... If a child is to keep alive [their] inborn sense of wonder... [they] need the companionship of at least one adult who can share it, rediscovering with him the joy, excitement and mystery of the world we live in."

—From *The Sense of Wonder*, by Rachel Carlson, written for her young nephew, Roger, about their explorations of her beloved Maine coast.

Creation Care Prayer

God, maker of marvels,
you weave the planet and all its
creatures together in kinship;
your unifying love is revealed
in the interdependence of
relationships in the complex world
that you have made.

Save us from the illusion that
humankind is separate and alone,
and join us in communion with all
inhabitants of the universe;
through Jesus Christ, our Redeemer,
who topples the dividing walls by
the power of your Holy Spirit,
and who loves and reigns with you,
for ever and ever.
Amen.

— Collect for the kinship and unity of all creation, from the Report to the 78th General Convention by the Standing Committee on Liturgy and Music. For more rich liturgical resources see also Anne Rowthorn and Jeffery Rowthorn, *God's Good Earth: Praise and Prayer for Creation* (Collegeville, MN: Liturgical Press, 2018).

Earth is crammed with heaven,
And every common bush afire with God;
But only [those] who see[s] takes off [their] shoes;
The rest sit round and pluck blackberries
And daub their natural faces unaware
More and more from the first similitude.

— Elizabeth Barrett Browning from Aurora Leigh

"It is these undeniable qualities of human love and compassion and self-sacrifice that give me hope for the future. We are, indeed, often cruel and evil. Nobody can deny this. We gang up on each one another, we torture each other, with words as well as deeds, we fight, we kill. But we are also capable of the most noble, generous, and heroic behavior."

"Any little thing that brings us back into communion with the natural world and the spiritual power that permeates all life will help us to move a little further along the path of human moral and spiritual evolution."

"Each one of us matters, has a role to play, and makes a difference. Each one of us must take responsibility for our own lives, and above all, show respect and love for living things around us, especially each other."

— Jane Goodall, *Reason for Hope: A Spiritual Journey*

Responding

- Read Jane Goodall's newest book, *The Book of Hope: A Survival Guide for Trying Times*. Listen to her "Hope Cast" at https://news.janegoodall.org/ and her interview with Krista Tippett, "What it Means to Be Human," on NPR's On Being https://onbeing.org/programs/jane-goodall-what-it-means-to-be-human/.

- The poetic form of haiku, is a simple way to witness the world around us and experience a connectedness to nature. Traditionally haiku have always included a seasonal word or phrase, a *kigo*, so that when you read the haiku you can place it in seasonal time: early spring, for example, or late fall, deep winter. This tradition prompts the poet to pay attention to the annual cycle of light and dark, growth and decline that affect all things, to see them in a journey we share with them. Haiku are not all about us humans, they are about creation, and our life in relationship to it. Here are two Haiku inspired by experiences in the memorial and peace garden at Trinity...

    priest stoops
    rubbing lavender's last blooms
    fall churchyard

    jewelweed
    hummingbirds probe
    each orange flask

Take time to observe the natural world around you. Perhaps take a walk in the woods, or walk barefoot on the grass or on a beach, or even dance in the rain. Sit quietly under an ancient tree, wait and watch and listen. Then write a haiku or two in response to what inspired you. Share them with the group. *– Sarah Strong*

- Find and read the "Canticle of the Sun" that is attributed to St. Francis. You can sing the text with hymn #406 or #407 (*The Hymnal 1982*). Better yet, listen to a musical setting of the text. There are many on the internet. For example, find a recording of "Missa Gaia" (Earth Mass) by the Paul Winter Consort. Even better, listen not only to the Canticle, listen to the entire Mass and other recording by Paul Winter that incorporate sounds from nature. Let it inspire your own Canticle to this earth, our fragile island home. Then look at our Eucharistic Prayer C (BCP, p. 369). This option was newly in the 1982 BCP, which is the same year the "Missa Gaia" was written. It was startling when first published. Share your reflections. Try writing a Eucharistic Prayer for today.

- In the Book of Common Prayer, beginning on p. 827 there is a set of Prayers for the Natural Order. Pray them together. In the next revision of our prayer book, what would you change given what has transpired in the last 40 years? Given what we know now, what is missing and what would you add? Why?

- Pay attention to the tradition of Rogation Days. Rogation comes from the Latin "rogare" meaning "to ask." They are celebrated Monday, Tuesday and Wednesday after Rogation Sunday, the 6th Sunday of Easter, or similarly the three days preceding Ascension. Collects for the three days are found in the BCP pp. 258-259. They are days of prayer and fasting and The Great Litany is often used. Typically, there has been a focus on the created world with blessings given for agriculture and industry and creation.

- Another time in the liturgical year that focuses on stewardship of the earth is the new tradition of Creation Season, September 1 to October 4. Now recognized by many faith groups world-wide, it is set aside as "a time for people of faith to renew the relationship with God and creation through celebration, prayer and action." You can find Episcopal resources here, though there are many other sites as well. https://www.episcopalchurch.org/publicaffairs/celebrate-the-season-of-creation/

Closing Prayer

Leader: God who called us into being, call us now to carry your word and work from this place into our lives and when we forget or ignore you…

All: Disturb us Lord!

When we linger where we are comfortable and do not journey into the harder path…

All: Disturb us Lord!

When we store treasures on earth and do not spread your bounty…

All: Disturb us Lord!

When we look at the person next to us and do not see your face in our neighbor…

All: Disturb us Lord!

When we see only stumbling blocks in our path and do not see what you are calling us to be…

All: Disturb us Lord!

Through your limitless Grace, **All: Open our hearts to what can be.**

Through your limitless Grace, **All: Open our arms to embrace your whole creation.**

Through your limitless Grace, **All: Remind us that all things are possible with you.**

> — Adapted by The Rev. George Sheats, from a prayer often incorrectly attributed to Francis Drake. This litany was composed for use at Trinity Church, Lewiston, ME, in a monthly Morning Prayer that is led by laity.

We thank you Almighty God, for the gift of water. Over it the Holy Spirit moved in the beginning of creation. Through it you led the children of Israel out of their bondage in Egypt into the land of promise. In it your Son Jesus received the baptism of John and was anointed by the Holy Spirit as the Messiah, the Christ, to lead us, through his death and resurrection, from the bondage of sin into everlasting life.

We thank you, [Holy One] for the water of Baptism. In it we are buried with Christ in his death. By it we share in his resurrection. Through it we are reborn by the Holy Spirit. Lead us we pray in living faithfully that which we have promised. In the name of the Incarnate One who calls us each by name. Amen.

> — *Thanksgiving Over the Water*, The Book of Common Prayer, *p. 305 (adapted)*

Appendices

PRAYING THE BAPTISMAL COVENANT

At some regular interval, perhaps on Ember Days, pray the Baptismal Covenant with this sheet.
Pause after each section and sit in contemplation of your life.
In the right-hand half of the page, note those things that come to mind.

Do you believe in God the Father, in Jesus Christ, the Son of God, and in God the Holy Spirit?
Our God,
it's one thing to say the creed
but another to put my trust in you.
Help me to live with the assurance that you are my Father
and that nothing can separate me from your love,
trusting in your forgiveness expressed in Jesus
and looking to your Spirit to make me your person.

Will you continue in the apostles' teaching and fellowship, in the breaking of bread, and in the prayers?
Our God,
I know I was not meant to go it alone
because you created the church
to be a supportive family for your children.
And I know the church is made up of people like me
—so it isn't perfect!
Help me to play my part in the church,
so I can learn from the teaching,
be encouraged by the fellowship,
be renewed in the Eucharist,
and find strength for living each day through prayer.

Will you persevere in resisting evil, and, whenever you fall into sin, repent and return to the Lord?
Our God,
You understand that sometimes
I do things I never intended to do.
My sorrow doesn't put it all right.
Neither can I use my weakness as an excuse.

Help me
to begin anew,
to experience your forgiveness
and to walk again in Jesus' way.

Will you proclaim by word and example the Good News of God in Christ?
Our God,
help me to live the way Jesus called me to live.
May my actions speak louder than my words
of your love and of new life in Jesus.
At the same time, help me rise above my own stumbling speech
and give me the words to express what I believe.
Let me be a witness to the Truth.

Will you seek and serve Christ in all persons, loving your neighbor as yourself?
Our God,
all too often I have looked at people
in a very superficial way.
Help me begin to see them with your eyes,
knowing that every person is created
in your image,
as your child.
If Jesus died for that person,
how can I despise him?
Give me a new love that reaches out to everyone
because Jesus died for all.

Will you strive for justice and peace among all people, and respect the dignity of every human being?
Our God,
I don't want my attitudes to be shaped
by the injustices that mar society,
by the discrimination, greed, and lust
that spoil relationships.
In Jesus
    color does not count,
    wealth carries no weight,
    and gender is not important.
Help me to live in Jesus,
to see people through his eyes,
and work for the harmony
that reflects your kingdom.

"Praying the Baptismal Covenant," by Reginald Hollis, c. 1993, may be reproduced with acknowledgment to Anglican Fellowship of Prayer.

A RITE OF PASSAGE

Aidan Kavanagh, once professor of liturgy at the Divinity School of Yale University, told the following story within a lecture delivered in August 1997 at the Theology Institute held at Holy Cross Abbey in Canon City, Colorado. It was printed in Liturgy 70 with Father Aidan's kind permission and is reprinted here to give both beauty and realism to our hopes for the Easter Vigil.

I have always rather liked the gruff robustness of the first rubric for baptism found in a late fourth-century church order which directs that the bishop enter the vestibule of the baptistery and say to the catechumens without commentary or apology only four words: "Take off your clothes." There is no evidence that the assistants fainted or the catechumens asked what he meant. Catechesis and much prayer and fasting had led them to understand that the language of their passage this night in Christ from death to life would be the language of the bathhouse and the tomb—not that of the forum and the drawing room.

So they stripped and stood there, probably, faint from fasting, shivering from the cold of early Easter morning and with awe at what was about to be consummated; years of having their motives and lives scrutinized; years of hearing the word of God read and expounded at worship; years of being dismissed with prayer before the Faithful went on to celebrate the Eucharist; years of having the doors to the assembly hall closed to them; years of seeing the tomb-like baptistery building only from without; years of hearing the old folks of the community tell hair-raising tales of what being a Christian had cost their own grandparents when the emperors were still pagan; years of running into a reticent and reverent vagueness concerning what was actually done by the Faithful at the breaking of bread and in that closed baptistery . . . . tonight all this was about to end as they stood here naked on a cold floor in the gloom of this eerie room.

Abruptly the bishop demands that they face westward, toward where the sun dies swallowed up in darkness, and denounce the King of shadows and death and things that go bump in the night. Each one of them comes forward to do this loudly under the hooded gaze of the bishop (who is tired from presiding all night at the Vigil continuing next door in the church), as deacons shield the nudity of the male catechumens from the women, and as deaconesses screen the women in the same manner. This is when each of them finally lets go of the world and of life as they have known it: the umbilical cord is cut, but they have not yet begun to breathe.

Then they must each turn eastwards toward where the sun surges up bathed in a light, which just now can be seen stealing into the alabaster window of the room. They must voice their acceptance of the King of light and life who has trampled down death by his own death. As each one finishes this, he or she is fallen upon by a deacon or a deaconess who vigorously rubs olive oil into his or her body, as the bishop perhaps dozes off briefly, leaning on his cane. (He is like an old surgeon waiting for the operation to begin.)

When all the catechumens have been thoroughly oiled, they and the bishop are suddenly startled by the crash of the baptistery doors being thrown open. Brilliant golden light spills out into the shadowy vestibule, and following the bishop (who has now regained his composure) the catechumens and the assistant presbyters, deacons, deaconesses and sponsors move into the most glorious room most of them have ever seen. It is a high, arbor-like pavilion of green, gold, purple and white mosaic from marble floor to domed ceiling sparkling like jewels in the light of innumerable oil lamps that fill the room with heady warmth. The windows are beginning to blaze with the light of Easter dawn. The walls curl with vines and tendrils that thrust up from the floor, and at their tops apostles gaze down robed in snow-white togas, holding crowns. They stand around a golden chair draped with purple upon which rests only an open book. And above all these, in the highest point of the ballooning dome, a naked Jesus (very much in the flesh) stands up to his waist in the Jordan as an unkempt John pours water on him and God's disembodied hand points the Holy Spirit at Jesus's head in the form of a white bird.

Suddenly the catechumens realize that they have unconsciously formed themselves into a mirror image of this lofty icon on the floor directly beneath it. They are standing around a pool set into the middle of the floor, into which gushes water pouring noisily from the mouth of a stone lion crouching atop a pillar at poolside. The bishop stands beside this, his presbyters on each side: a deacon has entered the pool, and the other assistants are trying to maintain a modicum of decorum among the catechumens who forget their nakedness as they crowd close to see. The room is warm, humid and it glows. It is a golden paradise in a bathhouse in a mausoleum: an oasis, Eden restored: the navel of the world, where death and life meet, copulate and become undistinguishable from each other. Jonah peers out from a niche, Noah from another, Moses from a third, the paralytic carrying his stretcher from a fourth. The windows begin to sweat.

The bishop rumbles a massive prayer—something about the Spirit and the waters of life and death—and then pokes the water a few times with his cane. The catechumens recall Moses doing something like that to a rock from which water flowed, and they are mightily impressed. Then a young male catechumen of about ten, the son of pious parents, is led down into the pool by the deacon. The water is warm (it has been heated in a furnace), and the oil on his body spreads out on the surface in iridescent swirls. The deacon positions the child near the cascade from the lion's mouth.

The bishop leans over on his cane and, in a voice that sounds like something out of the Apocalypse, says: "Euphemius! Do you believe in God the Father, who created all of heaven and earth?" After a nudge from the deacon beside him, the boy murmurs that he does. And just in time, for the deacon, who has been doing this for fifty years and is the boy's grandfather, wraps him in his arms, lifts him backwards into the rushing waters and forces him under the surface. The old deacon smiles through his beard at the wide brown eyes that look up at him in shock and fear from beneath the water (the boy has purposely not been told what to expect). Then he raises him up coughing and sputtering. The bishop waits until he can speak again, and leaning over a second time, tapping the boy on the shoulder with his cane, says: "Euphemius! Do you believe in Jesus Christ, God's only Son, who was conceived of the Virgin Mary, suffered under Pontius Pilate, and was crucified, died and was buried? Who rose on the third day and ascended into heaven, from whence he will come to judge the living and the dead?" This time the boy replies like a shot, "I do," and then he holds his nose . . . . "Euphemius! Do you believe in the Holy Spirit, the master and giver of life, who proceeds from the Father, who is to be honored and glorified equally with the Father and the Son, who spoke by the Prophets? And in one holy, catholic and apostolic church which is the communion of God's holy ones? And in the life that is coming?" "I do."

When he comes up the third time, his vast grandfather gathers him in his arms and carries him up the steps leading out of the pool. There another deacon roughly dries Euphemius with a warm towel, and a senior presbyter, who is almost ninety and is regarded by all as a "confessor" because he was imprisoned for the faith as a young man, tremulously pours perfumed oil from a glass pitcher over the boy's damp head until it soaks his hair and runs down over his upper body. The fragrance of this enormously expensive oil fills the room as the old man mutters: "God's servant, Euphemius is anointed in the name of the Father, Son and Holy Spirit." Euphemius is then wrapped in a new linen tunic; the fragrant chrism seeps into it, and he is given a burning terracotta oil lamp and told to go stand by the door and keep quiet. Meanwhile, the other baptisms have continued. When all have been done in this same manner (an old deaconess, a widow, replaced Euphemius's grandfather when it came the women's time), the clergy strike up the Easter hymn, "Christ is risen from the dead, he has crushed death by his death and bestowed life on those who lay in the tomb." To this constantly repeated melody interspersed with the psalm verse, "Let God arise and smite his enemies," the whole baptismal party—tired, damp, thrilled and oily—walk out into the blaze of Easter morning and go next door to the church led by the bishop. There he bangs on the closed doors with his cane; they are flung open, the endless vigil is halted and the baptismal party enters as all take up the hymn, "Christ is risen . . . ." which is all but drowned out by the ovations that greet Christ truly risen in his newly-born ones. As they enter, the fragrance of the chrism fills the church: it is the Easter-smell, God's grace olfactorally incarnate. The pious struggle to get near the newly baptized to touch their chrismed hair and rub its fragrance on their own faces. All is chaos until the baptismal party manages to reach the towering ambo that stands in the middle of the pewless hall. The bishop ascends its lower front steps, turns to face the white-clad neophytes grouped at the bottom with their burning lamps and the boisterous Faithful now held back by a phalanx of well-built acolytes and doorkeepers. Euphemius's mother has fainted and been carried outside for air.

The bishop opens his arms to the neophytes and once again all burst into "Christ is risen," *Christos aneste* . . . . He then affirms and seals their baptism after prayer, for all the Faithful to see, with an authoritative gesture of paternity – laying his hand on each head, signing each oily forehead once again in the form of a cross, while booming out: "The servant of God is sealed with the Holy Spirit." To which all reply in a thunderous "Amen," and for the first time the former catechumens receive and give the kiss of peace. Everyone is in tears.

While this continues, bread and wine are laid out on the holy table; the bishop then prays at great length over them after things quiet down, and the neophytes lead all to communion with Euphemius out in front. While his grandfather holds his lamp, Euphemius dines on the precious Body whose true and undoubted member he has become; drinks the precious Blood of him in whom he himself has now died; and just this once drinks from another special cup – one containing milk and honey mixed as a gustatory icon of the promised land into which he and his colleagues have finally entered out of the desert through Jordan's waters. Then his mother (now recovered and somewhat pale, still insisting she had only stumbled) took him home and put him, fragrantly, to bed.

Euphemius had come a long way. He had passed from death into a life he lives still.

SESSION MATERIALS

It is best if you compile all materials needed before beginning the first session.
As people in your parish for help in obtaining the items. Use the check off list below

Every Session

☐ Large glass bowl of water

☐ Long scarf or cloth

☐ Candle, matches

☐ Bible, *The Hymnal 1982*, The Book of Common Prayer—one for each person.
(Note that Living Water *cites the NRSV Bible, except for the psalms, which come from the Prayer Book Psalter; but use other translations as you see fit.)*

☐ Newsprint, markers

☐ Icon of the Baptism of Christ, or other thematic artwork, or photographs of baptisms

☐ Paper and pencils

☐ Audio media player

Session One

☐ Glass nuggets

☐ *The Message* by Eugene Peterson

☐ Pictures of fonts

☐ Watercolor paints and paper

☐ Recording: God Help Us

Session Two

☐ Selection of crosses, one per person

☐ Air-dry clay *(optional)*

☐ Images of God, Jesus, Holy Spirit

☐ Taizé songbook and/or audio media

Session Three

☐ Loaf of bread, basket

☐ Wheat, grapes *(optional)*

☐ Ingredients for unleavened bread *(optional)*

☐ Mural paper

☐ Markers

☐ Recording of sounds of water

Session Four

☐ Small, rough wood bowl or pottery bowl

☐ Shards of sea glass

☐ Recent newspapers

☐ Scissors, glue sticks

Session Five

- [ ] Small flask of oil
- [ ] Old magazines
- [ ] Scissors, glue sticks
- [ ] Votive candles, one per person

Session Six

- [ ] Hand towel
- [ ] Large, legible copy of "Hand-washing Prayer"
- [ ] Map of your neighborhood

Session Seven

- [ ] Pictures of people from around the world
- [ ] Print of Edward Hick's Peaceable Kingdom
- [ ] Drawings of Käthe Kollwitz
- [ ] Drawing paper and charcoal

Session Eight

- [ ] River rocks
- [ ] Bunches of small green branches
- [ ] Large copy of a blessing or two on newsprint

Epilogue

- [ ] Collection of leaves, berries, stones, flowers, pine cones, and other natural objects
- [ ] Copy of *The Sense of Wonder* by Rachel Carson, photographs by Nick Kelsh (New York: HarperCollins, 1998)

List other materials you choose to use:

SESSION PLANNING SHEET

Session Number:_____

Make one copy of this planning sheet for each session and use it for your notes on what you plan to do with the group and how you plan to accomplish it. Do your planning at least a week ahead of time. Check the appendix called "Session Materials" to be sure you have all the items you will need.

Notes on setting up the room:

GATHERING

Time: _____

How will you teach and lead the Opening Song? Do you need any recorded music?

Who will read the scripture passages and how? Who will lead the prayers?

What will you do as a time of greeting?

Session One: *you will need extra time for introductions, description of the process, plans for the coming sessions, and setting of norms.*

Sessions Two through Eight: *group check-in time, announcements, updates, responses to the previous session or insights gained since the last meeting.*

SHARING

Time: _____

Which story will you use? Who will read it?

How will you break into small groups?

REFLECTING

Time: _____

Which scripture passages will you use? Or will you break into small groups and let the groups choose their own passages?
Which of the quotes and poems will you use?   How will you structure the discussion time?

RESPONDING

Time: _____

Which of the suggested activities from "Practicing Together" will you use?
Do you need to gather any information or materials ahead of time?

Announcements about "homework" and plans for next session:

CLOSING PRAYER

Time: _____

Post Meeting Notes:

What went well? What would you do differently next time?

Is there anything you want to remember to return to in the next session?

Significant insights from the session:

GUIDELINES FOR GROUPS

by Marjory Zoet Bankson

1. Engage yourself in the process.
   Don't just observe.

2. Let Christ center the group.

3. Tell your own story.
   Emphasize experience over analysis.

4. Listen with your heart.
   Receive feelings and facts as given.
   Judge not.

5. Model by doing.
   Be vulnerable, open, affirming.

6. Give no advice!

7. Share time equally.

8. Honor the right to pass.

9. Practice confidentiality.
   Keep stories contained in the group.

10. Exercise your power to bless!
    Call forth one another's gifts.

11. Be accountable for your own growth.

12. We care. Christ cures.
    Pray for one another.

CPSIA information can be obtained
at www.ICGtesting.com
Printed in the USA
JSHW010750050722
27564JS00001B/3